geog.2

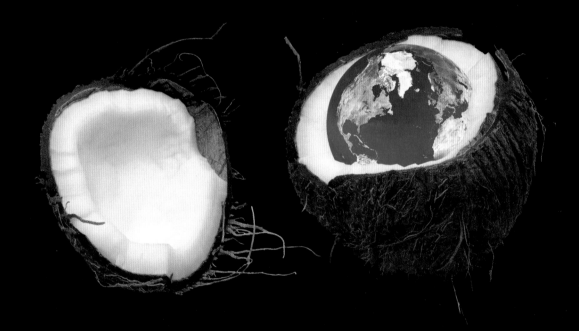

geography for key stage 3

<rosemarie gallagher><richard parish>

OXFORD

OXFORD
UNIVERSITY PRESS

Great Clarendon Street, Oxford OX2 6DP

Oxford University Press is a department of the University of Oxford.
It furthers the University's objective of excellence in research,
scholarship, and education by publishing worldwide in

Oxford New York

Auckland Cape Town Dar es Salaam Hong Kong Karachi
Kuala Lumpur Madrid Melbourne Mexico City Nairobi
New Delhi Shanghai Taipei Toronto

With offices in

Argentina Austria Brazil Chile Czech Republic France Greece
Guatemala Hungary Italy Japan Poland Portugal Singapore
South Korea Switzerland Thailand Turkey Ukraine Vietnam

Oxford is a registered trade mark of Oxford University Press
in the UK and in certain other countries

© RoseMarie Gallagher, Richard Parish 2008

The moral rights of the author have been asserted

Database right Oxford University Press (maker)

First published 2001
Second Edition 2005
Third Edition 2008

British Library Cataloguing in Publication Data

Data available

ISBN 978-0-19-913494-6

10 9 8 7 6 5

Printed in Singapore by KHL Printing Co. Pte Ltd.

Paper used in the production of this book is a natural, recyclable product made
from wood grown in sustainable forests. The manufacturing process conforms to
the environmental regulations of the country of origin.

Acknowledgements

The publisher and authors would like to thank the following for permission to use
photographs and other copyright material:

p4 Pavel Filatov/Alamy; p8l Corel/Oxford University Press; p8c&r Yann Arthus-Bertrand/Corbis UK Ltd.; p10tl Rolex Dela Pena/EPA; p10bl Paul Stover/Getty Images; p10tc Ian Leonard/Alamy; p10bc Robert Brook/Science Photo Library; p10tr Photofusion/Photographersdirect.com; p10br Peter Jordan/Alamy; p11l Keren Su/China Span/Alamy; p11c Sean Gladwell/Shutterstock; p11r Richard Packwood/Photolibrary; p12tl & bl Alamy Images; p12br Hideo Kurihara/Alamy; p12tr Renee Morris/Alamy; p15l & r Renee Morris/Alamy; p16 PictureLake/Fotolia; p17 Simmons Aerofilms; p19t Martin Bond/Environmental Images/Photofusion Picture Library; p19b Simmons Aerofilms; p20tl Daniel Gale/Shutterstock; p20ml Nickos/Fotolia; p20bl Stephen Hird/REUTERS; p20tc Hemera Technologies/Jupiter Images; p20mc Doug Houghton Art Directors and TRIP; p20tr Peter Titmuss/Alamy; p20mr Radius Images/Jupiter Images; p20br Keith Bowser Photography/Photographersdirect.com; p22 Geoff Tydeman/Fotolia; p23t Visit Cornwall; p23bl Robert Francis/Robert Harding/Photolibrary; p23br Getmapping/Global Mapping; p24t www.mike-page.co.uk; p24b www.mike-page.co.uk; p25l www.mike-page.co.uk; p25r www.mike-page.co.uk; p27tl Mike Page; p27tc David Moore/Alamy; p27tr Will Iredale/Shutterstock; p27b www.happisburgh.org.uk; p28 Hull News & Pictures Ltd/Photographersdirect.com; p29l www.mike-page.co.uk; p29r p27b www.happisburgh.org.uk/Jim Whiteside; p30 Alamy images; p32tl Andrew Fox / Alamy, p32lb Kathy deWitt / Alamy, p32rt Puchan/Shutterstock, p32rc Jonathan Ernst/REUTERS, p32br Beth Wald/Getty Images ; p33tl Clint Spencer/IstockPhoto , p33bl mb_fotos/CanstockPhoto, p33tr China Photos/Getty Images; p33br Craig Lenihan/Associated Press; p35 Elena Elisseeva/123rf; p36 Corel/Oxford University Press; p39tl, tc & br Corel/Oxford University Press; p39tr Jason Branz/Fotolia; p40t Stephen Hird/REUTERS; p40b Century Litho Limited; p41tl Gareth McCormack/Alamy; p41tr Corel/Oxford University Press; p41b David Hughes/123rf; p42 Adrian Muttitt/Alamy; p44t Paul Grover/Rex Features; p44b Phil Yeomans/Rex Features; p46t Peter Titmuss/Alamy; p46b Visuals Unlimited/Corbis; p47 Cordaiy Photo Library/Corbis UK Ltd.; p48 Norbert Wu/Minden Pictures/Getty Images; p49 Sean Burch/Associated Press; p52 Shutterstock; p54tl Robert Harding Picture Library Ltd / Alamy; p54tr Terry Heathcote/Oxford Scientific Films/Photolibrary; p54br Terry Heathcote/Oxford Scientific Films/Photolibrary Group; p54bl Kathie Atkinson/Oxford Scientific Films/Photolibrary; p57l Pete Oxford/Minden Pictures/Getty Images; p57c Buddy Mays/Corbis UK Ltd.; p57r Jupiter Images; p58tl Stephanie Maze/Corbis Uk Ltd.; p58tc Sue Cunningham/Worldwide Picture Library/Alamy; p58tr Edward

Parker/Alamy; p58b Martin Westlake/Alamy; p59tl Peter Bowater/Alamy; p59tr dublanko.com/Photographersdirect.com; p59b Earthshots/US Geological Survey; p60tl Pete Oxford, Danita Delimont/Alamy; p60tc Robert Harding Picture Library Ltd/Alamy; p60tr Craig Lovell/Eagle Visions Photography/Alamy; p60b David Hoffman Photo Library/Alamy; p61t Chris Stowers/PANOS, p61c Indo-Pacific Conservation Alliance; p61b Robert Simmon, Denelle Grant, Compton Tucker/NASA GSFC; p62t Wolfgang Kaehler/Corbis UK Ltd., p62c Pat & Tom Leeson/Science Photo Library; p62b Sumio Harada/Minden Pictures/Frank Lane Picture Agency; p63bl Steven J. Kazlowski/Alamy, p63bc Natural Visions/Alamy, p63br Joe McDonald/Corbis UK Ltd.; p63t blickwinkel/Alamy; p64t Bryan & Cherry Alexander Photography/Alamy, p64b Jacques Langevin/Sygma/Corbis UK Ltd.; p65t Bryan & Cherry Alexander Photography/Alamy, p65b Alexander Zemlianichenko/AP/Empics; p66t Bryan & Cherry Alexander Photography/Alamy; p66c Alaska Stock/Photolibrary; p66b Jacques Langevin/Sygma/Corbis UK Ltd; p67t Geophotos; p67b Rinie Van Meurs/Foto Natura/MINDEN PICTURES/Getty Images; p68 Adrian Arbib/Alamy; p70t Mircea Bezergheanu/Shutterstock; p70b Maximilian Weinzierl/Alamy; p71 Radius Images/Jupiter Images; p78 Photographersdirect.com; p79l Dita Alangkara/Associated Press; p79r Ed Wray/Associated Press; p80 Andrew Milligan/PA/Empics; p84l IstockPhoto; p84r Sergei Grits/Associated Press; p85l Jonas Jordan/U.S. Army; p85r Diaphor La Phototheque/Photolibrary; p87tl Ace Stock Limited/Alamy; p87tc Paul Felix Photography/Alamy; p87tr Index Stock Imagery/Photolibrary; p87ml Paul Glendell/Alamy; p87mc Pelamis Wave Power; p87mr Marine Current Turbines TM Limited; p87b Cyril Hou/Shutterstock; p88t Jim West/Alamy; p88b Skyscan Photolibrary/Alamy; p89t PCL/Alamy; p89b Spectrum Photofile Inc./Photographersdirect.com; p90l Dave Ellison/Alamy; p90c Chris George/Alamy; p90r Agencja Fotograficzna Caro/Photographersdirect.com; p91l Colin Palmer Photography/Alamy; p91r Paul Glendell/Alamy; p92tl Corbis; p92tc Scott Olson/Getty Images; p92tr Scott Olson/Getty Images; p92bl Rex Features; Eurelios/Science Photo Library; p95l Charles Sturge/Alamy; p95r Danita Delimont/Alamy; p96l & r National Renewable Energy Laboratory; p97tl, tr & b National Renewable Energy Laboratory; p98 Alamy Images; p100t Jackie Chapman/Format Photographers/Photofusion Picture Library; p100b Joanne O'Brian/F Photographers/Photofusion Picture Library; p101 CR World; p102 London Aerial Photo Library; p105tl Michael Yamashita/Corbis UK Ltd.; p105tc & cr London Aerial Photo Library; p105tr Barnaby's Picture Library; p105cl Inge Yspreet/Corbis UK Ltd; p105c Martin Sookias/Oxford University Press; p105bl Purcell Team/Corbis UK Ltd; p105bc Mark Edwards/Still Pictures; p105br Art on File/Corbis UK Ltd; p107t Martin Sookias/Oxford University Press; p107b CR World; p108tl Gallo Images/Paul Velasco/Corbis Uk Ltd.; p108tc Martin Sookias/Oxford University Press; p108tr Dominic Burke/Alamy; p108b Oxford University Press; p109t Martin Sookias/Oxford University Press; p109m Barnaby's Picture Library; p109b Roger Bamber/Alamy; p110tl Tom Brakefield/Corbis UK Ltd; p110tc Jonathan Blair/Corbis UK Ltd; p110tr Stone/Getty Images; p110t Gardel Bertrand/Photolibrary; p110c Sean Sprague/Alamy; p110cr Massimo Listri/Corbis UK Ltd; p110bl Jamil Bittar/REUTERS; p110br Michael & Patricia Fogden/Minden Pictures/Getty Pictures; p112l Yann-Arthus-Bertrand/Corbis UK Ltd.; p112tr Ecoscene/Joel Creed/Corbis UK Ltd; p112cr Marco Simoni/Photolibrary; p112br Corel/Oxford University Press; p108tl Corel/Oxford University Press; 108tr Luiz C Marigo/Photolibrary; p108bl Stephanie Maze/National Geographic/Getty Images; p108bc Luiz C Marigo/Photolibrary; p108br Mediacolor's/Alamy; p115l Jacques Jangoux/Photolibrary; p115c David Hartley/Rex Features; p115rt Ricardo Beliel/BrazilPhotos/Alamy; p115rb Andre Penner/Associated Press; p116 Daniel Laire/Corbis UK Ltd; p117 Stephanie Maze/Corbis UK Ltd; p118 David R. Frazier Photolibrary Inc./Alamy; p120t Mike Goldwater/Alamy; p120b Christopher Pillitz/Getty Images; p121t Georgphoto/Photographersdirect.com; p121c Paulo Fridman/Corbis; p121b Andresr/Shutterstock; p123 Victor R. Caivano/Associated Press; p124t the Image Bank/Getty Images; p124b Purcell Team/Corbis UK Ltd; p126t Renato Chalu/Associated Press; p126bl Alvian Pungki/REUTERS; 126bc Nigel JH. Smith/Photolibrary; p126br Fernando Bueno/Getty Images; p127tl MISR Team, NASA/GSFC/LaRC/JPL; p127tr Celso Junior, AE/Associated Press; p127b Corel Professional Photos; p128t Food and drink photos/Photolibrary; p128bl Rickey Rogers/REUTERS; p128br Alexandre Meneghini/Associated Press; p130 ABP/Dinodia; p132t Stephen Mulcahey/Alamy; p132b Museum of London; p133t Christine Osborne Pictures/Alamy; p134l Comstock/Jupiter Images; p134c Peter Titmuss/Alamy; p134tr Tom Cummins/Shutterstock; p134cr Parbul TV via Reuters TV (BRITAIN); p134br David Noble Photography/Alamy; p135l Alan Copson City Pictures/Alamy; p135c Mike Booth/Alamy; p135r Bernd Tschakert/Alamy; p136tr Jyothi Joshi/Shutterstock.

The OS map extracts on pp. 23, 25 and 91 are reproduced with the permission of the Controller of Her Majesty's Stationery Office © Crown Copyright. The map on page 73 is reproduced with the permission of the Intergovernmental Panel on Climate Change. The London Underground Tube map on page 136 is reproduced with the permission of Transport for London (registered user no 08/1183/P). The map on page 26 was provided by Catherine Poulton, British Geological Survey.

Illustrations are by James Alexander, Alan Baker, Barking Dog Art, Jeff Bowles, Stefan Chabluk, William Donohoe, Michael Eaton, Jeff Edwards, John Hallet, Hardlines, Tim Jay, Roger Kent, Richard Morris, David Mostyn, Tim Oliver, Colin Salmon, Martin Sanders, and Tony Wilkins.

We thank all who helped during research for this book. In particular, and in topic order: Diana Wrightson and Malcolm Kerby of Coastal Concern Action Group (Happisburgh); James Lovelock; Jack Stone of the National Renewable Energy Laboratory, USA; Akanksha Chaurey of the Tata Energy Research Institute, New Delhi; Dr Nick Fyfe of the Department of Geography, University of Dundee; Chris Morris, GIS Analyst at Brent Council; Phil Spivey and Martin Garrad of the Community Safety Department, Sussex Police; Jane Oakland of Wembley Police; Nelson Lafraia of the Brazilian Embassy, London; Silvia and Penny Aldersley; William F Laurance, Smithsonian Tropical Research Institute, Balboa, Panama.

We thank our excellent reviewers for their thoughtful and constructive criticism: Stephen Kaczmarczyk, Anna King, Phyl Gallagher, John Edwards, Katherine James, Roger Fetherston, and Mike Gallagher.

We thank Janet Williamson for her contribution to this book, and her overall contribution to the geog.123 course.

Cover photo: Getty Images (globe).

Every effort has been made to contact copyright holders of material reproduced in this book. Any omissions will be rectified in subsequent printings if notice is given to the publisher.

Contents

1 People and the planet

The big picture

This chapter is about us and our planet. These are the big ideas behind the chapter:

◆ The number of people on the Earth is growing fast.

◆ We are not spread evenly around the Earth. Some places are very crowded, and some are quite empty.

◆ The more of us there are, the more resources we use: land, water, fuels, and so on.

◆ In fact we are competing with each other for resources.

◆ We are competing with other living things too: both plants and animals. The more of us there are, the less room for them.

Your goals for this chapter

By the end of this chapter you should be able to answer these questions:

◆ Roughly how many people are on the Earth right now? And how is this number changing?

◆ What do these terms mean?

birth rate   death rate   population distribution   population density

◆ What kinds of things affect a country's birth and death rates?

◆ Which parts of the world are the most crowded, and which are the most empty?

◆ Is there a link between population distribution and climate? If so, can I explain it?

◆ We depend on the Earth's resources. What examples can I give? (At least three.)

◆ We have harmed our planet. What examples can I give? (At least three.)

And then …

When you finish this chapter, come back to this page and see if you have met your goals!

Did you know?
◆ Around 360 000 new babies are born every single day.

Did you know?
◆ The world's population is expected to reach 8 billion by 2025.
◆ It was 6 billion in 2000.

What if …
◆ … the number of people on the Earth kept on growing and growing?

What if …
◆ … we ran out of land to live on?

Your chapter starter

Look at the photo on page 4. What's the woman doing?

Do you ever eat those things in the bucket?

The photo has lots of clues about how we use our planet. How many can you find?

Suppose *you* had to choose a photo, to show how we use our planet. What kind of photo would you choose?

I want more.

Here you'll discover how quickly our numbers are rising – and why.

Here we go !

200 000 years ago   2000 years ago   200 years ago   Today

How does the population rise so fast?

As you can see above, the number of humans on the Earth is rising fast. This is the story of one family …

Bo and Ella fell in love. They got married and had **4** children.

All 4 of these had children of their own. **18** altogether.

16 of the 18 in turn had children of their own – **76** altogether.

So Bo and Ella's family just kept on growing.
It has been like this all over the world, for centuries.
So it's easy to see how the population has risen so fast.

But what about deaths?

Every year, millions of humans die. But the population still keeps rising!

For example in 2007, about 53 million people died. From old age, disease, injuries, and poverty.

But far more new babies were born that year – about 132 million altogether.

So the world population grew by about 79 million that year. This was an increase of about 1.4%.

Your turn

1 What does *population* mean?

2 The Earth's population grew slowly at first. Now it is growing really fast. Look at this table.

How the human race has grown

Year	Population (billions)
10 000 BC	0.004 (which is 4 million)
5000 BC	0.005 (or 5 million)
1000 BC	0.05 (or 50 million)
1 AD	0.2 (or 200 million)
1000	0.3 (or 300 million)
1600	0.5 (or 500 million)
1800	1.0 (or 1000 million)
2000	6.0 (or 6000 million)

a What was the population in the year 1000?

b What was it in the year 1800?

c The population was much larger in 2000 than in 1800. How many times larger?

3 A graph is a great way to show how the population is growing. One is started below:

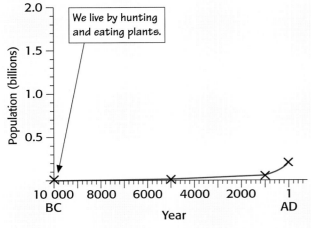

Look at the lower axis of the graph. What does each tiny division on it represent? Choose one:

a 50 years   b 100 years   c 200 years

4 Now *you* have to draw the graph. Like this:

a Make a *large* copy of the axes started above. Use a full page, or even two pages joined together. Continue the lower axis to **2400 AD**. Continue the side axis up to **8 billion**.

b Plot the eight points from the table above.

c Join the points with a smooth curve. Do your best!

d Give your graph a title.

5 Look at your graph.

a Write a sentence to describe its shape.

b If the Earth's population keeps growing like this, about what will it be by the year 2200?

c Explain how you arrived at your answer for **b**.

6 Adding notes to a graph helps to bring it alive. So now you can add notes to your graph, from the box below. (The graph in **3** has an example to help you.)

At this year ...	write this ...
10 000 BC	We live by hunting and eating plants.
9000 BC	The first farms appear.
7500 BC	The first towns appear.
4500 BC	The wheel is invented.
3000 BC	The first cities appear, and the first writing.
1000 BC	The Iron Age starts. (We begin using iron for ploughs and other tools.)
43 AD	The Romans invade Britain.
400 AD	The Romans leave Britain.
1750 AD	The Industrial Revolution starts. (We begin using engines, and build lots of factories.)
?	I was born.

7 From your graph you will see that these helped the population to grow faster. See if you can explain why.

A the discovery of iron

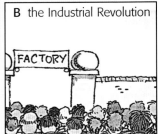
B the Industrial Revolution

8 The Earth's population is rising fast, overall. But in some countries the population is rising slowly, or even falling!

a First, find out what these terms mean. (Glossary?)

   i birth rate   ii death rate

b Now look at these two lists.

1	Changes in a country
a	Everyone gets better food to eat.
b	A terrible war breaks out.
c	A deadly disease spreads.
d	There is a severe famine.
e	More hospitals and doctors are provided.
f	Birth control pills are provided.
g	More women take up good jobs.

2	Possible results
A	Death rate rises.
B	Death rate falls.
C	Birth rate rises.
D	Birth rate falls.
E	No effect on birth or death rates.

For each change in list **1** choose the likely result(s) from list **2**. (You can choose more than one result.) Write your answer as a complete sentence, like this: *If everyone gets better food to eat, then ... .*

So where is everyone?

In this unit you'll see how we are spread unevenly around the world – and explore some reasons why.

From empty to crowded

Some places, like Antarctica, are empty. People only visit.

Some parts are lightly populated. For example much of Australia.

Some parts are very crowded. Like Mexico City.

The world's population distribution

This map shows how we are spread or **distributed** around the world. The deeper the red, the more crowded the area is. Or, in other words, the higher its **population density**. What can you say about the UK?

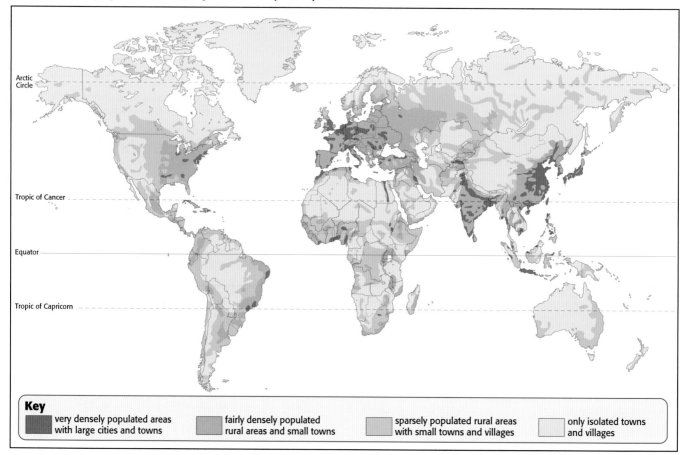

Arctic Circle

Tropic of Cancer

Equator

Tropic of Capricorn

Key

very densely populated areas with large cities and towns

fairly densely populated rural areas and small towns

sparsely populated rural areas with small towns and villages

only isolated towns and villages

Your turn

The world map on pages 140 – 141 will help with these.

1 All these terms appear on page 8. See if you can explain what they mean. (Use the glossary only if you get stuck.)
   a densely populated   b sparsely populated
   c population distribution d population density

2 Which two *continents* have the largest areas of very high population density?

3 Name two *countries* that are:
   a very crowded, overall   b very lightly populated

4 Overall, where do more people tend to live?
   a in the middle of continents
   b on or near the coast
   See if you can come up with a reason for this.

5 Climate affects all living things. It is one reason why some regions are less crowded than others.
   a What's the climate like, at A on the map below?
   b This shows what crops need:

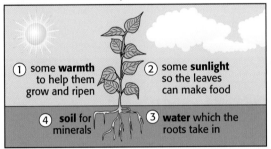

① some **warmth** to help them grow and ripen
② some **sunlight** so the leaves can make food
④ **soil** for minerals
③ **water** which the roots take in

Will crops grow well at A? Give reasons.
   c Is the population density at A high, or low? Give as many reasons as you can to explain why.

6

Place	Country	Climate	Population density	Reasons
B				

a Make a table like the one started above, but larger. Leave room to write quite a lot in the last column.
b Write the letters B, C, D and E from the map below, in the first column.
c Name the countries they're in, in the second.
d Describe the climate at each place, in the third column. (Use the key, and things you know already.)
e In the fourth column describe the population density at each place, using one of these phrases:
   very high   fairly high   fairly low   very low
f In the last column give as many reasons as you can, to explain why the population density is like this. The map on page 51 may help too.

Key

Hot tropical rainy climates
- rain all year
- monsoon
- dry in winter

Very dry climates
- no reliable rain
- a little rain

Cold polar climates
- no warm season and fairly dry

Warm summers, mild winters
- dry in summer (Mediterranean climate)
- dry in winter
- no dry season

Cool climates
- rain all year
- dry in winter

Mountain climates
- the higher you go, the colder it gets

The world's climate regions

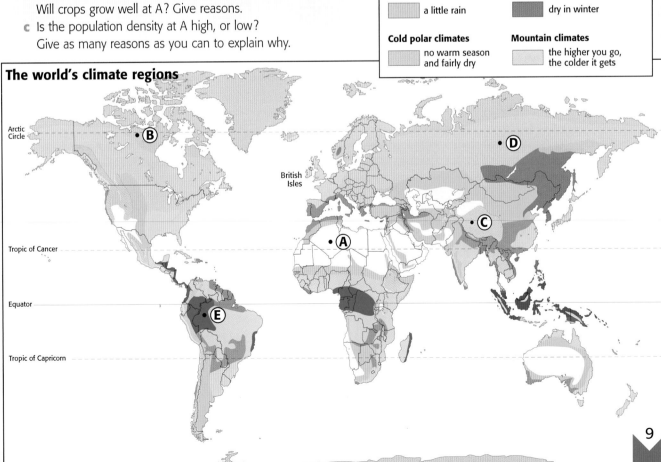

Arctic Circle
British Isles
Tropic of Cancer
Equator
Tropic of Capricorn

Our impact on our planet

This unit is about the impact of our growing population on our planet.

Growing fast

As you saw earlier, our numbers are growing fast.

Look at this population graph. It's like the one you drew in Unit 1.1. Look how the line shoots up.

Just think. There are about 210 000 more of us on the Earth now than this time yesterday.

By this time next year, there will be around 80 million more.

Do you think that might cause problems? Like what?

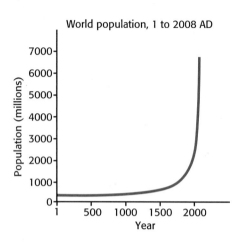

World population, 1 to 2008 AD

The demand for resources

The more of us there are, the more of the Earth's **resources** (land and materials) we use up. For example, the more of us there are …

… the more food we need, to feed us all …

… and the more homes we need – huts, flats, houses …

… and the more fuel – oil, coal, gas, petrol, electricity, firewood …

… which means more land cleared for farming, and more minerals dug up to make fertiliser.

… which means more land cleared for homes, and more timber, stone, clay, and sand used up.

… which means more trees gone, and more land cleared for oil and gas wells, coal mines, power stations.

There are so many of us that we even compete with each other for resources. There have already been wars over land, and oil! Some people predict that one day, quite soon, there will be wars over fresh water.

Our impact on the Earth

We are the cleverest species on the Earth. We make use of its resources in all kinds of ways. But it's not all good news.

The more land we take over, the less is left for all the other living things. We think that over 100 000 species a year are dying out now. Even pandas are in danger!

The more resources we use, the more waste we create. It gets dumped on land, and at sea. Some rots away quite fast. But some will hang around for centuries.

We cause other pollution too. Like **acid rain** that kills trees (above). And scientists say we're helping to bring on **global warming**, by burning so much coal, oil, and gas.

Those are just some of the ways we harm our planet.
The larger the population, the greater our impact will be.

In Chapter 4, you can read about our impact in two special places: the tropical rainforests and the tundra. Chapter 5 has more on global warming.

So is there no hope?

There is hope.

- We see now that we must live in a more **sustainable** way. That means in a way that does not harm us, or other species, and is not wasteful.
- We are trying to repair some of the damage we've done.
- Experts say our population will not keep growing. Some predict it will rise to 9 billion by 2050, then fall. (It's falling in some countries already.)

What if ...
- *... we each looked after our part of the planet really really well?*

Did you know?
- *In 1979, China made a rule that women should have no more than 1 child each.*

Your turn

1 These are some of the Earth's resources:
water soil wood metal ores oil
Choose just two of them, and say how you depend on them. Give your answers as spider maps, like this:

food crops I eat, such as rice and beans

I depend on soil because it is needed to grow...

cotton, that I wear

2 Look at the resources listed in **1**.
   a Which of them would you die without? Explain why you chose this / these, and not the others.
   b Which could we run out of? Explain your choice.

3 *Pandas feed on bamboo. Once there were plenty of pandas in the bamboo forests of Vietnam and China. But the forests were cut down for farming, and to make way for towns. Now there are only about 1600 pandas left on the Earth.*
Think about this. Then make up a conversation between a panda mum and her baby, about humans and their babies.

4 Suppose the human population doubles in the next 50 years. What problems do you think that might cause:
   a for humans like you?   b for other animals?
(Don't forget things like waste, and sewage.)

5 Look at this idea.
Do you agree with it?
Give your reasons.

ONLY ONE CHILD PER FAMILY FROM NOW ON!

2 Coasts

▲ Stoer, Scotland.

▲ Morston Marshes, Norfolk.

▲ Sennen Beach, Cornwall.

▲ The Seven Sisters, Sussex.

SCOTLAND

NORTHERN IRELAND

REPUBLIC OF IRELAND

WALES

ENGLAND

The big picture

This chapter is all about the **coast**, where the land meets the sea.
These are the big ideas behind the chapter:

◆ The coast is shaped and changed by the waves – and by humans !

◆ The waves shape it by eroding, transporting and depositing material. This gives special landforms.

◆ We humans change it by how we use it. (For example, for seaside resorts.)

◆ Along some of the coast, where the rock is soft, the sea is eroding land and homes away.

◆ There are ways to slow down this erosion. But they all cost a lot.

Your goals for this chapter

By the end of this chapter you should be able to answer these questions:

◆ What causes waves ?

◆ How do waves shape the coast ?

◆ What do these terms mean ?

   erode   transport   deposit   longshore drift

◆ What are these, and how are they formed ?

   beach   bay   headland   cave   arch   stack   stump
   wavecut platform   spit   salt marsh

◆ In what ways do we use the land along the coast?
   Give at least five examples.

◆ Why is the coastline eroding fast, in some parts of the UK ?

◆ What can we do, to protect land and homes from coastal erosion ?

◆ Why can't we protect *all* the places that are at risk of erosion ?

◆ What is the government's strategy, for fighting coastal erosion ?

And then ...

When you finish the chapter, come back to this page and see if you have met your goals !

Did you know?
◆ Part of our south coast is called the Jurassic coast ...
◆ ... because lots of dinosaur remains are found there.

Did you know?
◆ The UK's coastline is 12 430 km long.
◆ That's over twice the distance from London to New York.

What if...
◆ ... rising seas drowned half our coast?

What if...
◆ ... Britain had no coast?

Did you know?
◆ 8 of the world's 10 largest cities are on a coast.

Your chapter starter

Page 12 shows places on our coast.

What's the coast ?

What can you do there ?

How far do *you* live from the coast ?

Why does it look so different in different places ?

Has anyone seen my flippers?

In this unit you'll learn what causes waves and tides, and begin to find out how waves affect the coast.

What causes waves?

Waves are caused by the **wind** dragging on the surface of the water.
The length of water the wind blows over is called its **fetch**.

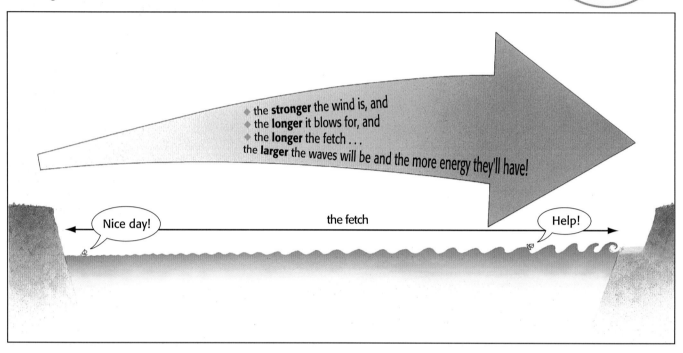

When waves reach the coast

Out at sea, the waves roll like this. In a gale they can be over 30 metres high!

They break in shallow water, like this. The water that rushes up the sand is called the **swash**.

The water rolling back into the sea, like this, is called the **backwash**.

If the backwash has more energy than the swash, the waves eat at the land, dragging pebbles and sand away. (This happens with high steep waves.) But if the swash has more energy than the backwash, material is carried on to the land and left there. (This happens with low flat waves.)

Tides

Even when the sea is calm and flat, the water level is always changing. That's mainly because of the moon. As the moon travels around the Earth, it attracts the sea and pulls it upwards. (The sun helps too. But it is much further away so its pull is not so strong.)

The rise and fall of the sea gives us the **tides**. Look at these photos:

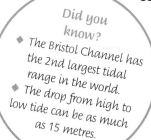

Did you know?
◆ The Bristol Channel has the 2nd largest tidal range in the world.
◆ The drop from high to low tide can be as much as 15 metres.

Tuesday 9.00 am. The tide is **in**, here at Wells in Norfolk. In fact the sea has reached its highest level for today. This is called **high tide**.

Same day, 3.20 pm. Now the tide is **out**, leaving the boats resting on the mud. The sea has fallen to its lowest level for the day. This is called **low tide**.

High tides occur about every twelve and a half hours, with low tides in between. The drop in sea level from high to low tide is called the **tidal range**. It keeps changing, because the pull on the sea keeps changing as the moon moves around the Earth, and the Earth around the sun.

Your turn

1 Which three factors determine how high the waves in a place will be?

2 The arrows are winds blowing onto island X.

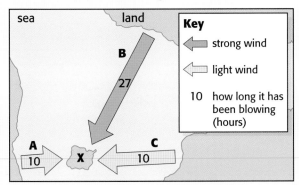

sea   land

Key
→ strong wind
⇐ light wind
10 how long it has been blowing (hours)

B
27
A
10 X C 10

Which wind will produce:
a the largest waves   b the smallest waves
at the coast of X? Explain your answers.

3 Now think about the waves around your own island.
a The *prevailing wind* in the UK is a *south west wind*. What do the terms in italics mean? (Glossary?)
b Explain why the south west tip of England gets some really high waves. (Check pages 140 –141.)

c Most of the UK's surfing schools are in south west England, and Wales. Suggest a reason.

4 Using a full sentence, explain what these terms mean:
a swash
b backwash

5 Look at the photos on page 12.
a Which beach do you think has stronger backwash, C or D? What is your evidence?
b Which of the four places probably gets hardly any waves? How did you decide?

6 a What are *tides*, and why do they occur?
b Photo B on page 12 was taken at low tide. How would the scene look different, at high tide?
c Now repeat b for photo C.
d Look at photo D. Was this taken at high tide? How can you tell?

7 Now look at photo A on page 12. You are on holiday in Scotland. Two days ago you were scrambling around on the rocks – and got trapped at **X** by high tide! Write a really exciting entry for your diary saying how you felt, and how you were saved.

The waves at work

In this unit you'll learn how waves shape the coastline.

What do the waves do?

Waves work non-stop, night and day, year after year, shaping the coastline. This shows what they do.

1 They wear away or **erode** the coast. These cliffs are being eroded. (Some of the rock has already been **weathered** – broken down by weather and plants.)

3 They drop or **deposit** it in sheltered areas where they lose energy.

2 They carry away or **transport** the eroded material.

Now we will look at each of these in more detail.

Erosion

This is how waves wear away the coast:

They pound at the rock like a hammer. Over time, this breaks the rock up.

They force water into cracks in the rock. That helps to break it up. It's called **hydraulic action**.

They dissolve soluble material from the rock. This is called **solution**.

Chunks of rock get knocked together and worn into smaller and smaller bits. This is called **attrition**. They end up as **shingle** (pebbles) and **sand**.

They fling sand and pebbles against the rock. These wear it away like sandpaper. This is called **abrasion**.

The more energy the waves have, and the softer the rock, the faster erosion will be.

Transport

The waves carry the eroded material away. Some is carried right out to sea. But a lot is carried *along* the coastline. Like this …

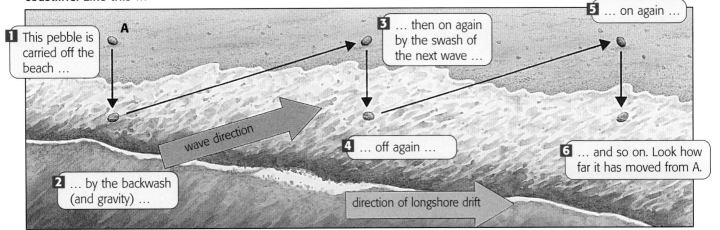

1 This pebble is carried off the beach …

2 … by the backwash (and gravity) …

3 … then on again by the swash of the next wave …

4 … off again …

5 … on again …

6 … and so on. Look how far it has moved from A.

wave direction

direction of longshore drift

In this way, hundreds of thousands of tonnes of pebbles and sand get moved along our coastline every year. This movement is called **longshore drift**.

Many seaside towns build **groynes** to stop their beaches being carried away by longshore drift. Look at this photo.

Deposition

Waves continually carry material on and off the land. If they carry more *on* than *off* – a beach forms!

Beaches form in sheltered areas. Low flat waves carry material up the beach and leave it there. Some beaches are made of sand, and some are **shingle** (small pebbles).

a groyne

N

▲ *The groynes stop the beach being carried away.*

Your turn

1 Waves do three jobs that shape the coastline. Name them.

2 Describe three ways in which waves erode rock.

3 These two pebbles are made of the same rock.
   a Which one has been in the water for longer? Explain.
   b Name the process that made Y so smooth.

X   Y

4 Groynes are barriers of wood or stone, on a beach. Look at the groynes in the photo above.
   a Why were they built?
   b Are they working? How can you tell?
   c From which direction do the waves usually arrive at this beach?
     i from the south west
     ii from the south east
     Give your evidence.

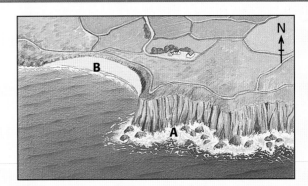
N
B
A

5 This drawing shows part of an island (not Britain).
   a The *prevailing wind* for the island is blowing. From where does it blow? (Look at the waves!)
   b There is no beach at A. Suggest a reason.
   c There is a good beach at B. Give a reason.
   d Where might the sand at B have come from?

6 Do you think the rock around our coast all erodes at the same rate? Give your reasons.

Landforms created by the waves

In this unit you will learn about the landforms that the waves create along the coast, by eroding and depositing material.

Sculptor at work !

This coast is made of different rocks, some hard, some soft.
Once upon a time it was straight. Just look at it now !

cave
arch
stack

1 Hard rock erodes more slowly than soft rock.
So now, cliffs of hard rock jut out, forming a **headland**.

3 Here the softer rock has been eroded away, leaving a **bay**.

4 Another headland. Here you can see a **cave**, an **arch** and a **stack**.

2 At the base of these cliffs is a **wave-cut platform**.

How a wave-cut platform forms

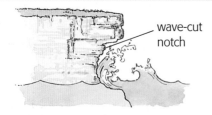

wave-cut notch

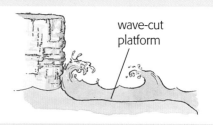

wave-cut platform

1 The waves carve **wave-cut notches** into cliffs at a headland. These get deeper and deeper …

2 … until, one day, the rock above them collapses. The sea carries the debris away.

3 The process continues non-stop. Slowly the cliffs retreat, leaving a **wave-cut platform** behind.

How caves, arches and stacks form

cave

arch

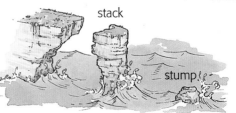

stack

stump

1 The sea attacks cracks in the cliff at a headland. The cracks grow larger – and form a **cave**.

2 The cave gets eroded all the way through. It turns into an **arch**. Then one day …

3 … the arch collapses, leaving a **stack**. In time, the waves erode the stack to a **stump**.

6 Some is deposited in sheltered areas like this one, forming a **beach**.

7 Here the coast bends to form a bay with calmer water, which interrupts the longshore drift …

10 Silt and mud may build up in this sheltered area. It becomes a **salt marsh**.

9 The end of the spit is curved by the waves.

salt marsh

spit

5 Eroded material is carried along the coast by longshore drift.

8 … so sand and shingle are deposited here, in the sea. They build up a **spit**.

Your turn

1

Landform	Created by ...	
	erosion	deposition
headland	✓	

Make a table like the one started here. Write in the names of all the landforms you met in this unit. Then put a ✓ to show how each was formed.

2 Make a larger sketch of the landforms in photo A.
  a On your sketch, label:
    a wave-cut notch   an arch   a stump
  b Explain how the arch was formed.
  c Draw a dotted line to show where there was once another arch.
  d What will happen to the stump over time?

3 Photo B shows the spit at Dawlish Warren in Devon.
  a Make a sketch of the spit. Don't forget to show and label the groynes, and salt marsh areas.
  b Now, a challenge. From which direction does the prevailing wind blow, at Dawlish Warren? How did you decide? Mark the direction on your sketch.

4

coast (seen from above)   N

Key
- soft rock
- hard rock
- very hard rock
- prevailing wind

sea

This shows some coast before erosion. Make a larger drawing to show how it may look 10 000 years from now. Label any landforms, and annotate (add notes to) your drawing to explain what has happened.

A

B

We use the coast in many different ways. Here you can find out about them.

What do we use the coast for?

You saw how the waves change the coast. Now what about us?
How do we change it? What do we use it for? Look at these photos.

A

It's great to get away.

B

This used to be a huge industry in the UK.

Not now.

C

That lot is just in from China.

D

Baaa.

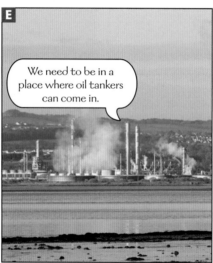

E

We need to be in a place where oil tankers can come in.

F

We moved here for the view.

G

Atten-shun!

H

We take sand and gravel from the sea bed, off the coast.

Millions of tonnes a year ...

...for things like road building.

Who owns it?

So who owns our coastline?

◆ Over half of it belongs to the state (55%).

◆ About 3% belongs to the Ministry of Defence.

◆ The National Trust has bought 1100 km of coastline. To give us all access to it, and protect it from development. It wants to buy more.

◆ Perhaps 20% is in the hands of private owners. For example farmers. It is hard to get exact figures.

◆ Local councils own the rest.

Did you know?

◆ You can own land along the coast – but not under the sea.

◆ All the sea bed, in the UK's waters, belongs to the state.

Your turn

1

There are lots of settlements along our coast: villages, towns and cities.
a Many early settlers chose to settle on the coast. Why? Give as many reasons as you can.
b Now underline any reasons that you think may still apply, for people living on the coast today.

2 Look at the photos on page 20. They show ways we use the land at the coast, and the sea off it.
You have to match each photo to a term in the box below. But the terms are all jumbled. So you must sort them out first. (Start with the easy ones?)

mesho	deesias storres	fragnim
dustriny	gredding	hisginf
trops	feendec	

Give your answer like this: **A =**

3 Now look at this list of the UK's largest cities.
a Some have ports, which helped them to grow. Which ones? The map on page 139 may help.
b How many other ports can you name, in the UK? Try for *at least* two.

4 Most of us love the seaside.
a How many seaside resorts can you name, in the UK? Try for *at least* four.
b A challenge. See if you can draw a sketch map of the British Isles, *from your mental map*, and mark those seaside resorts on it!

5 Look again at the photos on page 20. People are at work in all those places – even if you can't see them. They work in different **sectors** of the economy. Which of the photos could be used to illustrate:
a the primary sector?
b the secondary sector?
c the tertiary sector?
Explain your choices. (Try the glossary if you are stuck.)

6 Now see if you can name *at least* five jobs that people can do on the coast or at sea, but not inland.

7 The UK is one of the world's richest countries – even if it does not seem rich to you! Its coast has helped to make it rich. See if you can explain how. (Think about what you learned in history?)

8 Are there any *disadvantages* in having a coastline? See if you can come up with some. Answer in any way you choose. (Spider map? drawings? bullet points?)

9 So, would you like to live on the coast? Yes or no? Explain why.
(Or, if you live on the coast already, say how you feel about living there, and why.)

The UK's 10 largest cities

	Name	Population (millions)
1	London	7.17
2	Birmingham	0.98
3	Leeds	0.72
4	Glasgow	0.58
5	Sheffield	0.51
6	Bradford	0.47
7	Edinburgh	0.45
8	Liverpool	0.44
9	Manchester	0.44
10	Bristol	0.38

In this unit you'll find out about Newquay, in Cornwall, with the help of an OS map.

Meet Newquay

Look at the OS map opposite. It shows Newquay, on the coast of Cornwall.

400 years ago, Newquay was just a small fishing village. Then it became a port for shipping tin, and clay, and lead, out of Cornwall. Now it's a seaside resort – and a surfers' paradise.

And you are going there on holiday.

Your turn

1 Look at the OS map and photos. What do they tell you about the coast at Newquay? Is it flat? Smooth? Any beaches? See if you can write four sentences about it.

2 Find Towan Head on the map. (It's at 7962.)
   a What is *Head* short for?
   b How was Towan Head formed?
   c Find two other examples of this landform on the map. Give their names.
   d What can you say about the rock in those places?

3 Photo **A** shows a tiny island. It's at 811618 on the map, near the aquarium. Do you think it was always like this? Explain.

4 Look at photo **B**. It shows some of Newquay's beaches. See which ones you can name, with help from the map.

5 Now, holiday time. You are off to Newquay on a five-day camping holiday, in August, with your friends.

I'm hungry. I'm tired. Hurry up, you lot.

   a They let you pick a camp site, from the map. Which one will you choose? Give a 6-figure grid reference for it, and say why you chose it.
   b The map gives plenty of clues about things to see and do, in Newquay. List as many as you can. Then tick the ones that appeal to you.
   c You will go there by train. Where is the station? Give a 6-figure grid reference for it.
   d From the station, you'll go straight to the tourist information office, to find out about surfing lessons.
      i About how far is the office from the station?
      ii In which direction will you walk?

6 You book some surfing lessons. They will be at Lusty Glaze beach. (It's a good place for beginners.)
   a You will walk to lessons from your camp site. See if you can draw a sketch map of your route. Mark in any landmarks, and say how long the route is.
   b Lessons will start at 9 in the morning. What time do you think you'll need to leave the camp site?

7 You see lots of other surfers. They (and other people) fly into Newquay from London, Leeds, Bristol, Dublin, Alicante, Zurich, and other cities.
   a Find Newquay airport on the map. Give a grid reference for one square of it. (It uses St Mawgan airfield, which once belonged to the RAF.)
   b There are plans for a big increase in the number of flights to and from Newquay, in the future.
      i In what ways will this benefit Newquay? List as many as you can.
      ii What problems might it cause?
   c A change is *sustainable* if it helps us economically, and socially, without harming the environment. So we will not regret it later.
      i Overall, do *you* think an increase in flights is sustainable? Give your two main reasons.
      ii Would you agree to it, if you were in charge of Newquay?

8 Home again. Now you are going to write a blog about Newquay, for your web page. Say where it is, and what it's like, and what you did. Make it fun! What photos will you add to your page? And what about a map?

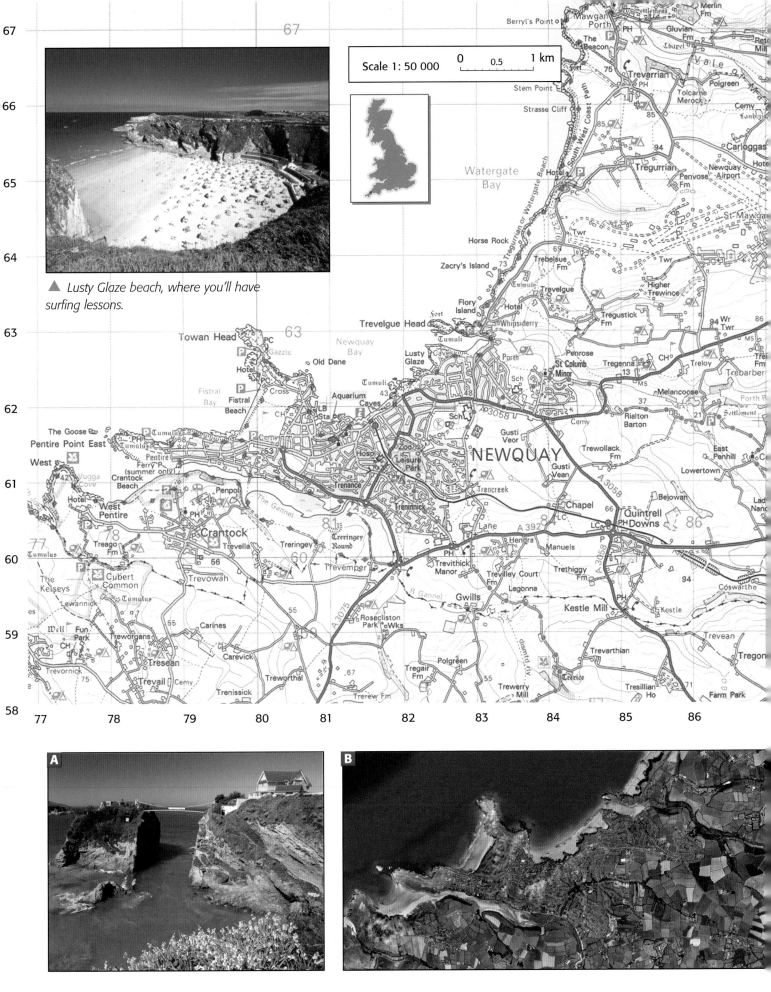

▲ Lusty Glaze beach, where you'll have surfing lessons.

Scale 1 : 50 000

0   0.5   1 km

How long can Happisburgh hang on?

North
Sea

The Wash

Happisburgh

In this unit you'll see how erosion by the waves is causing big problems in one coastal village, in Norfolk.

Waiting for the sea to arrive

Diana Wrightson has a great view of the sea, from her home on Beach Road, in Happisburgh, in Norfolk. (Pronounce it *Haisbro*!)

But she does not know how much longer she can stay there. A few months? A year? A few years? It depends on the sea.

Because the sea is already eating at her back garden. Not so much, in summer. But in winter, when stormy north winds blow, big chunks can disappear. And one day, her house will go too. It's only a matter of time.

'We had big plans to do the house up', said Diana. 'But now there's no point. And we can't sell it – it's worth nothing! And unless things change, we'll get no compensation either, when it topples over the cliff. It's all a big worry.'

The people next door have abandoned their house already. Diana does not want to leave until she really has to. As winter draws near, she will watch the sea nervously. How much longer has she got?

From a conversation with Diana Wrightson, June 2008

▲ *Diana Wrightson's house (⊙) on Beach Road. Look for it on the photo below.*

Why is erosion so severe at Happisburgh?

7 These wooden barriers (or **revetments**) were meant to slow down erosion, by making the waves break early. But they were destroyed in a past storm.

Beach Road

1 The main problem is that the cliffs are soft – sand on top and clay below.

2 Rain soaks into the cliffs and helps to weaken them. (This is one form of **weathering**.) The more rain they hold, the weaker they get.

3 Meanwhile, the sea erodes the cliffs from below. Not so much in summer, when the weather is calmer …

4 … but winter often brings strong north winds, and storms. Big waves batter the cliffs, and big chunks of them collapse.

6 Groynes help to slow down erosion. (They stop sand being carried away, and the sand absorbs some of the waves' energy.) But they can't prevent it.

5 A line of big rocks, called **rock armour**, has been put in to protect the cliffs from the full force of the waves. It works – but there isn't enough of it.

Your turn

1 What part does each play in the threat to Diana's house?
  a the material the cliffs are made of
  b rain
  c strong north winds blowing down the North Sea

2 Now look at the aerial photos below. They show Happisburgh in 1996 and 2007.
  a What are all the white objects near the top of each photo? (The OS map on the right will help.)
  b In which compass direction was the camera pointing?
  c Look at the wooden barriers on both photos.
    i What are the ones at right angles to the cliffs called? What is their job?
    ii What are the ones parallel to the cliffs called? What is their job?
    iii On the second photo, you can clearly see another type of barrier too. What is it called?

3 a Now list all changes you notice for that stretch of coast, between 1996 and 2007.
  b From the photos, do you think any of those barriers:
    i prevented erosion? ii slowed it down? Explain.

4 Even with barriers, the cliffs at Happisburgh are eroding at a rate of about 2 m a year. Where there are no barriers, the rate is about 8 m a year.

Suppose the barriers remain as in the second photo below. Based on this OS map, say how long you think it will be before the sea reaches:
  a the church
  b the lighthouse (which is not shown in the photos)

Scale 1cm : 250m

▲ Happisburgh in 1996. Look how far from the sea Diana's house was then.

▲ Happisburgh in 2007. Look how many houses have gone since 1996 – and the sea won't stop there.

The war against the sea

In this unit you'll find out where on our coast erosion is a problem, and what we can do about it.

It's not just Happisburgh!

In the last unit you saw that erosion is a big problem in Happisburgh. (Say *Haisbro*.) But it's not the only place.

The blue lines along the coast on this map show the main stretches that suffer from erosion. Here the sea is busy eating land away, and stealing people's homes.

Rock types in the UK

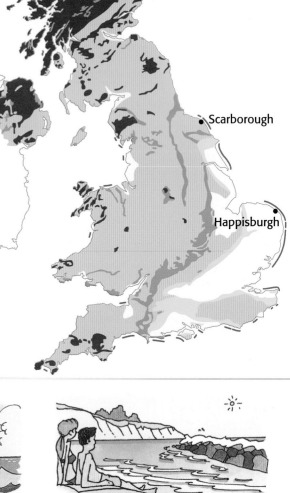

Scarborough

Happisburgh

Key

Rock types

■	very hard	igneous and metamorphic
▨	hard	limestone
▨	medium	sandstone and mudstone
▫	fairly soft	chalk
□	soft	soft sediments
⌒	where coastal erosion is a problem	

So how can we stop coastal erosion?

Where there are waves, there will be erosion. So we can't *really* stop it. But we can slow it down. By building **defences** that will hold the waves back, or reduce their energy.

Look at these examples. You've met most of them already.

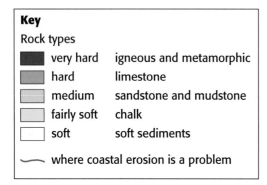

You could build **sea walls** like this one, to stop the waves reaching valuable land …

… or a barrier of **rock armour** (big rocks) to soak up their energy. Less energy means less erosion.

You could even build a **reef** of rocks out at sea, so that the waves break away from the beach.

You could try wooden **revetments**. The waves batter them, instead of the cliffs.

You could build **groynes** to stop sand being carried away. Sand absorbs some of the waves' energy.

You could even add more sand or shingle to a beach, to build it up. It's called **beach replenishment**.

But it's not that simple …

So, we *can* slow down coastal erosion. In that case, why are places like Happisburgh being eaten away so fast? It all comes down to money.

First, coastal defences cost a lot. Rock armour like this costs about £2500 per metre. Sea walls cost about £5000 per metre.

And they don't last forever. Look at these revetments at Happisburgh, destroyed in a storm. So you have to keep on spending.

Also, **global warming** is causing sea levels to rise. And causing more storms. So you must keep on building bigger, stronger, defences.

… so Happisburgh suffers

The photo on page 24 shows groynes and revetments at Happisburgh. These were built over 40 years ago. They broke down several times, and the local council repaired them. Now they are in bad shape.

For a long time, the local people have been asking for new defences. But most of the money for new defences has to come from the government. And the government said no!

People have kept on fighting for them. Some emergency rock armour was put down, to gain time. It was paid for by the council, and donations. But it is not enough.

So what will become of Happisburgh now? And the other places at risk from the sea? Find out more in the next unit.

▲ *Campaigning for coastal defences, outside Parliament.*

Your turn

1 Look at the map on page 26.
 a Where in the UK is most of:
  i the very hard rock? ii the soft rock?
 b Does the map show a link between rock type and erosion? Describe what you notice.

2 You need to tell someone (who can't see the map) where on the coast erosion is a problem. Write down what you will say.

3 Look at the ways to slow down erosion, on page 26.
 a Which *two* do *you* think might work best? Explain your choice.
 b Which one do you think would be least good? Why?
 c Which (if any) will last forever? Explain.

4 Around 850 people live in Happisburgh village. You are one of them. Write a letter to a newspaper, saying *why* the government should protect Happisburgh.

5 You want to plan new defences for Happisburgh, to show the government. The little OS map on page 25 will help.
 a Show your plan as a sketch map. Mark in the length of each defence you choose. (Check the OS scale.)
 b Add brief notes to your map, to explain your choice.
 c Now work out the cost, using this list:

Cost of coastal defences

Sea wall	£5000 per metre
Rock armour	£2500 per metre
Sea reef (42 metres long)	£2 million
Wooden revetment	£1500 per metre
Typical rock groyne	£125 000
Typical wooden groyne	£100 000
Beach nourishment	£10 per cubic metre

27

What will the government do, about protecting places from the sea?
You can find out in this unit.

The defence dilemma

As you saw, Happisburgh is being eaten by the sea. And it is not alone.
Many other places around the coast are suffering too. So they all want
sea defences that really work. It's a big dilemma for the government:

So, who will get help?

The government has decided that some places will be protected from the
sea. And some won't.

What about Happisburgh?

Sadly, Happisburgh will not get money for new defences.
It is a small village, with a population of about 850.
Defences would cost more than the homes and land are
worth. So they will be left to slip into the sea.

Now look for Scarborough on the map on page 26. It is a
busy seaside town, with a population of about 106 000.
It will continue to be defended. But one day, if sea levels
keep on rising, even Scarborough may have to go.

Scarborough got new sea defences in 2005. Cost: £53 million. ▶

What next for the people of Happisburgh?

The Happisburgh people are angry that their village will be let go.
And they think they should get compensation.

- The government won't defend us from the sea ...
- ... so it must compensate us when we have to move out.
- It's only fair.
- If we knew we'd get money, we would not worry so much.
- We could buy a house in a safer place.
- Now the houses along here are worth nothing.
- And it's not even our fault.

What do *you* think?

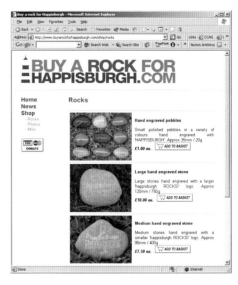

▲ *Raising money for Happisburgh, to buy more rock armour.*

Your turn

1 Do you agree with this person? Explain.

WE MUST NOT let the sea take any more homes.

2 The map on the right shows the plans for defending the north coast of Norfolk (where Happisburgh is).
 a Some of the coastline will not be defended. What do you think is the main reason?
 b Name two villages that won't be defended.

3 a Cromer will continue to be defended, at least for now. Using clues from the map, suggest a reason. Say which clues you used.
 b Sea Palling has fewer than 600 people. But it will be defended. See if you can find a reason for this, from the map.
 c Winterton won't be defended. What questions would you ask about it, to understand why?

4 a What is *compensation*? (Glossary?)
 b Suppose the government agrees to compensate people who lose their homes to the sea. Where will *it* get the money from?
 c Here's one person's opinion. What do you think? Give your opinion, and reasons.

They chose to live there. Why should they get compensation?

5 You live on Beach Road in Happisburgh. (See page 24.) You want to sell your house NOW. But no one will buy it, because of the cliff erosion. What will you do? See if you can come up with a plan.

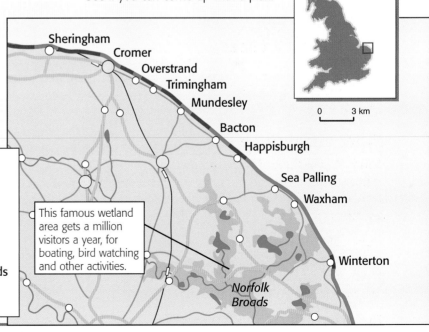

Key

▬ defend the coastline, at least for now	▪▪▪ main road
▬ let the sea take over	— secondary road
◯ town	— railway
○ village	🌿 The Norfolk Broads National Park (protected area)

Sheringham
Cromer
Overstrand
Trimingham
Mundesley
Bacton
Happisburgh
Sea Palling
Waxham
Winterton

0   3 km

This famous wetland area gets a million visitors a year, for boating, bird watching and other activities.

Norfolk Broads

3 Weather and climate

The big picture

This chapter is all about **weather** and **climate**. These are the big ideas behind the chapter:

◆ Weather is the state of the atmosphere around us. (Warm ? wet ? windy ?) It can change from hour to hour.

◆ The main causes of weather are the sun, and water vapour.

◆ Climate is the 'average' weather in a place – what it is *usually* like there.

◆ Climate changes from place to place, because of factors such as distance from the equator, and from the sea.

◆ The Earth can be divided into different climate regions.

Did you know?
◆ The wettest place in the world is Cherrapunji in India (1270 cm of rain/year).

Your goals for this chapter

By the end of this chapter, you should be able to answer these questions:

◆ What does this term mean?

*temperature   precipitation   air pressure   wind speed
wind direction   cloud cover   visibility*

◆ What are the three different kinds of rainfall, and how does each form?

◆ What kind of weather is linked with:

low pressure ?   high pressure in summer ?   high pressure in winter ?

◆ The weather in the UK can change very quickly. Why ?

◆ What do these terms mean ?

air mass   warm front   cold front

◆ In the UK, storms are usually caused by depressions. What's a depression?

◆ What's the difference between weather and climate?

◆ What's a climate graph, and how do I draw one ?

◆ What factors influence climate? And which is the main one?

◆ The Earth can be divided into regions with very different climates. Which examples can I give? (At least four!)

Did you know?
◆ The lowest ever recorded temperature was –89.2 °C, in Antarctica, on 21 July 1983.

What if …
◆ …the weather was the same every single day ?

What if …
◆ …the climate was exactly the same all over the world?

And then …

When you finish the chapter, come back to this page and see if you have met your goals !

Your chapter starter

Look at the photo on page 30.

What's the white stuff ?

What caused it ?

How would it feel to be there ? What kinds of things could you do ?

What might this place look like in six months' time ?

Out, penguin.

It's the weather!

In this unit, you'll think about different kinds of weather.

Hot, cold, wet, dry, windy?

It's all around you. It affects what you wear, and what you do, and how you feel. You can't control it. It's the weather!

Look at the photos, and then try 'Your turn'.

Your turn

1 Look at each photo in turn. What's the weather like in that place? Give one to four words to describe it. For example *very cold, snowy*.

2 Now choose the two photos that you think show:
   a the most similar weather
   b the most 'opposite' weather
   Each time, explain your choice.

3 From the photos, you must choose one place to be in, on that day, in that weather.
   a Which place will you choose? Why?
   b Which one would be your very last choice? Why?

4 Which of the photos do you think were *not* taken in the UK? Explain your choice.

5 Can weather be dangerous? If you think so, give examples. The photos may help.

6 a So what exactly *is* weather? See if you can write a definition for it. All in your own words!
   b Now compare your definition with the one in the glossary. Which one do you think is better? Why?

7 And finally, a challenge. What do you think *causes* weather? See if you can come up with some suggestions. (No peeking in any books.)

So what causes weather?

In this unit you'll learn about the two main causes of weather.

Two main causes

Weather has two main causes, **the sun**, and **water vapour**.
The sun is the most important one.

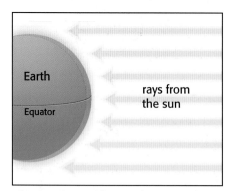

The sun heats the Earth. But it does not heat it evenly, because the Earth is round. So the top and bottom don't warm up much.

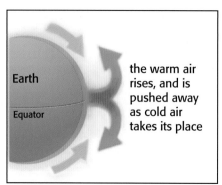

The Earth in turn heats the air – so the air also warms unevenly. Warmer air rises. Colder air then moves in to take its place, as **wind**.

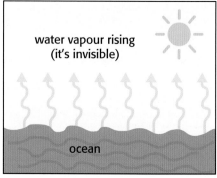

The sun also warms the oceans. This causes water to evaporate to give a gas, **water vapour** – the second main cause of weather.

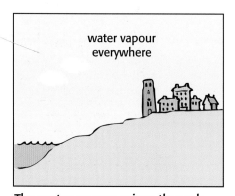

The water vapour mixes through the air, helped by wind. So there is some in the air around you, even if you are miles from water.

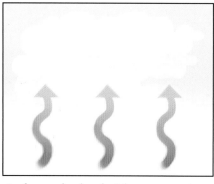

And now look what happens when air rises. It cools, which causes the water vapour to condense again, into **clouds** of tiny water droplets.

The droplets may join to form heavier drops, which then fall from the sky as rain. (We also call this **precipitation**.)

If the air is very cold, the water droplets may fall instead as **hailstones**, or **sleet**, or **snow**. It all depends on the air temperature.

Water vapour may also condense lower down in the air. For example in chilly weather, it may condense all around us as **fog**.

Or it may hang in the air as **mist**. Or condense on cold grass and leaves overnight, as **dew**. These evaporate again in the sunshine.

Other factors that influence weather

So, the sun and water vapour are the two main causes of weather. They lead to warmth, wind, rain, snow, hail, sleet, fog, mist, and dew.

But many other factors *influence* the weather, and the **climate** (the kind of weather a place usually gets). For example, places beside the sea are cooled by sea breezes, in summer.

These other factors make the weather very different, in different places. You can read about them in Unit 3.9.

So where does weather happen?

Look up at the sky. You are looking into the atmosphere: the blanket of gas around the Earth.

The atmosphere is divided into layers. Most of the gas molecules that make up the air are in the lowest layer, thanks to gravity. This lowest layer is called the troposphere. It is 11 km deep, on average.

The troposphere is the layer that gets warmed by the Earth. And it has almost all the water vapour. So it is the layer where most weather occurs. Fly above it, and you won't find rain.

▲ Jet planes often fly in the stratosphere. It saves fuel. Can you guess why?

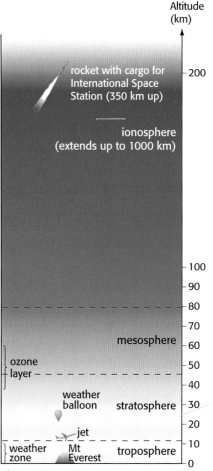

▲ The layers of the atmosphere.
The troposphere is where we live – and where you get weather.
Weather balloons can rise to 35 km.
We use them to measure temperature and pressure in the stratosphere.

Your turn

1 When we think of weather, we think about how warm or cold it is, or wet, or cloudy, or windy.

Copy and complete this paragraph, using words from the brackets below.
Places get warm because of the _____. It heats the _____, and the Earth in turn _____ the air. The sun also causes _____. That's because the warm air _____, so _____ air rushes in from somewhere else to take its place. Rushing air is called wind. During our _____ there is not much sun, so the weather can be _____.
(*winter   wind   chilly   cooler   Earth   rises   sun   warms*)

2 What is *water vapour*? How does it get into the air?

3 See if you can think of a way to prove there is water vapour in the air today. (Hint: a very cold surface?)

4 For each weather condition below, say which you think is the most likely cause, *the sun*, or *water vapour*:
a hot   b windy   c cloudy   d rain   e hail

5 In the UK, it is hotter in June than in December. See if you can explain why.

6 a How high up does the troposphere reach?
b There's no rain in the stratosphere. Why not?

35

Measuring the weather

In this unit you will find out how the weather is measured – and how to read a simple weather map.

Looking is not enough

Weather is the state of the atmosphere at a given time. You can tell a lot about it just by looking.

But to describe it fully, you need to ask questions like these. And answer them by measuring!

All around the world, night and day, the different aspects of the weather are measured. At weather stations on land, and by special equipment on planes, ships, weather balloons, and in satellites.

Then **meteorologists** or weather scientists use the data to write weather reports, and draw weather maps, and make weather forecasts.

Your turn

1 Look at the weather map on the right. Below are symbols it uses. Say what you think each means. (The key will help!)

a   b

c   d

e   f   (27)

g   (20)   h   16

2 The photo above shows Seaburn on the day the weather map was drawn. Find it on the weather map.
   a Using the map to help you, describe the weather around Seaburn that day as fully as you can, giving some data.
   b Was it warm or cold there, that day? Say why you think so.

3 Now say what you think the weather was like at:
   a X on the weather map   b Y on the weather map

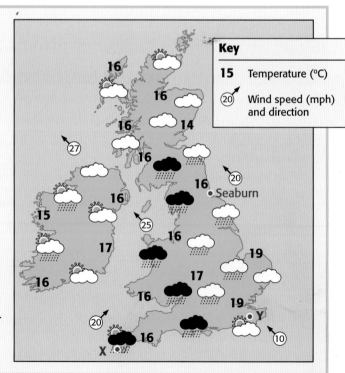

Key

15	Temperature (°C)
(20) ↗	Wind speed (mph) and direction

Weather term	Means ...	Usually given ...	Measured using ...
temperature	exactly how hot or cold it is		
	how 'heavy' the air is	in millibars (mb)	
	how much of the sky is hidden by clouds		your eyes
	how fast the wind is blowing		
	where the wind is blowing from (a south west wind blows from the south west)	as a compass bearing (N, NW, SW and so on)	
	water falling from the sky in any form (rain, hail, sleet, snow)		
	how far ahead we can see, for example on a foggy day	in metres or kilometres	

4 This question is all about measuring the weather.
You will need to do a little detective work.
(The glossary will help.)

  a First, make a copy of the table above.

  b In the first column of your table, write each term from list **A** below, in the correct place.

  c Complete the third column using list **B**.
Start with the easiest units.

A Weather terms	**B** Units
wind direction	kilometres or miles
air pressure	per hour (like a car)
precipitation	millimetres per day (or
wind speed	month or year)
visibility	oktas
cloud cover	degrees Centigrade (°C)

5 Now look at box **C**. It shows equipment for measuring the weather. Look at each item in turn. What do you think it measures? Write its name in the correct place in the fourth column of your table.

6 Some days are very cloudy. **Cloud cover** means how much of the sky is hidden by cloud. You can tell by looking. It is measured in eighths or oktas, like this:

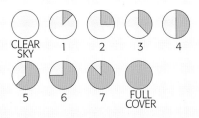

CLEAR SKY 1 2 3 4 5 6 7 FULL COVER

  a Now look at the photo on page 36. As far as you can tell from a photo, what do you think the cloud cover was at Seaburn that day? Answer in oktas.

  b Do the same for the photo on page 30.

7 a Look back at your table. Which of those aspects of the weather could you measure at home?

  b Choose one. Say *how* you would measure it, and *when*. Draw a diagram to show any equipment you'd use, and where you would place it.

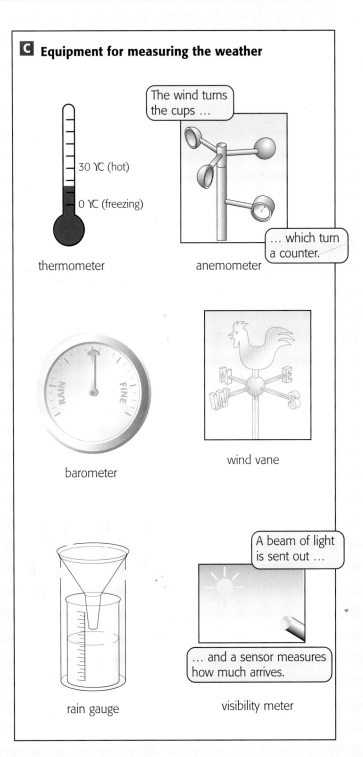

C Equipment for measuring the weather

The wind turns the cups ...

30 ℃ (hot)

0 ℃ (freezing)

thermometer

... which turn a counter.

anemometer

barometer

wind vane

A beam of light is sent out ...

... and a sensor measures how much arrives.

rain gauge

visibility meter

More about rain and clouds

Here you'll learn about three types of rainfall, and some different kinds of cloud.

Three types of rainfall …

All rain is caused by air rising, and its water vapour condensing.
But the air can rise for different reasons – so we give rain different names.
Let's look at the three main types of rainfall.

1 Convectional rainfall

Here the air rises because the ground heats it.

It rises as currents of warm air.
We call these **convection currents**.
So we call the rain **convectional rainfall**.

In the UK we get convectional rainfall inland in summer, where the ground gets hottest, away from the cooling effect of the sea.

3 The rising air cools.
The water vapour condenses.
Clouds form. It rains.

2 Currents of warm air rise.

1 The sun warms the ground … which then warms the air above it.

2 Relief rainfall

Wind is moving air.

When the wind meets a line of high hills or mountains, there's only one way to go – up ! So the air rises and cools – and we get rain. We call it **relief rainfall**.

In the UK the prevailing wind is from the south west. So we get a lot of relief rainfall on the high land along the west coast.

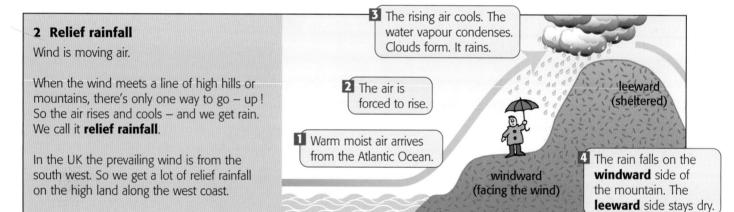

3 The rising air cools. The water vapour condenses. Clouds form. It rains.

2 The air is forced to rise.

1 Warm moist air arrives from the Atlantic Ocean.

leeward (sheltered)

4 The rain falls on the **windward** side of the mountain. The **leeward** side stays dry.

windward (facing the wind)

3 Frontal rainfall

As you'll see in Unit 3.6, huge blocks of air called **air masses** move around the Earth.

When a warm air mass meets a cold one, the warm air is forced to rise. So we get rain. This is **frontal rainfall**.

Frontal rain can fall anywhere, since air masses can travel anywhere. In the UK, they often arrive in from the Atlantic Ocean. So the west of the UK gets a lot of frontal rain.

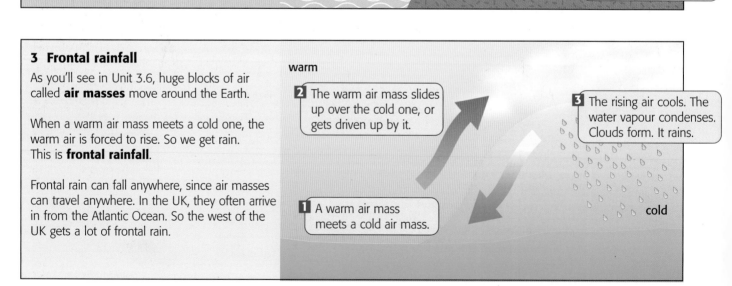

warm

2 The warm air mass slides up over the cold one, or gets driven up by it.

3 The rising air cools. The water vapour condenses. Clouds form. It rains.

1 A warm air mass meets a cold air mass.

cold

... and some different types of cloud

Clouds are all just water droplets. But they have different shapes.
The shape depends on things like how fast the air rose, and how
much wind there is. Here are the three main cloud types:

cumulus clouds

stratus clouds

cirrus clouds

Fluffy clouds. They form low in the sky and can bring short, heavy showers. (Some grow into tall dark clouds that bring very heavy rain.)

Big blankets of dull cloud. They hang low in the sky, and can cover it all. They can give drizzle, but not heavy showers.

Thin wispy high clouds (over 6 km up). It's freezing up there, so they are made of ice crystals! They can mean bad weather is on the way.

Cumulus clouds are usually the result of warm air rising fast. For example when the ground heats the air quickly on a hot day, or air rises at the side of a mountain. (See **1** and **2** on page 38.)

Stratus clouds are the result of air rising more slowly, over a wide area. For example when a warm air mass slides up slowly over a cold one, leading to frontal rain. (See **3** on page 38.)

Cirrus clouds are usually an early sign that a warm front is arriving.

Your turn

1 Which type of rainfall is caused by a warm air mass meeting a cold one?

2 Why is *relief rainfall* called that? (*Relief* is in the glossary.)

3 To form clouds, two things are always needed. Which are they? Choose from this list:
   wind   rising air   mountains   hot sun
   warm ground   water vapour

4 Do you think clouds can form in the dark? Explain.

5 Name a type of cloud which:
   a is made of ice crystals
   b forms a dull blanket and gives drizzle.

6 Look at this photo. It was taken on a hot afternoon. Two hours earlier, there were no clouds to be seen.
   a Which kind of clouds are they?
   b What do you think caused them to form?

7 Look at the map on page 139. The Cambrian mountains get a lot of rain. Explain why.

6 August 1 pm.

Air pressure and weather

This unit is about air pressure, and the kind of weather high and low pressure bring.

What's air pressure?

Although we can't feel it, all the air above us is pressing down on us, giving **air pressure**. If air pressure is **low**, it means air is rising. If it is **high** it means air is sinking. And each brings different weather.

Low pressure weather

Look again at what happens when warm air rises:

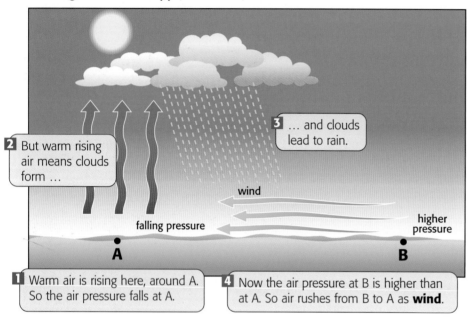

2 But warm rising air means clouds form …

3 … and clouds lead to rain.

wind

falling pressure

higher pressure

A

B

1 Warm air is rising here, around A. So the air pressure falls at A.

4 Now the air pressure at B is higher than at A. So air rushes from B to A as **wind**.

So the fall in air pressure at A is a sign of rain and wind. The lower the pressure, the worse the weather will be.

▲ *Low pressure weather in summer. In winter, you could get heavy snow instead of rain.*

High pressure weather

When warm air rises in one place, cool air sinks somewhere else – giving high pressure.

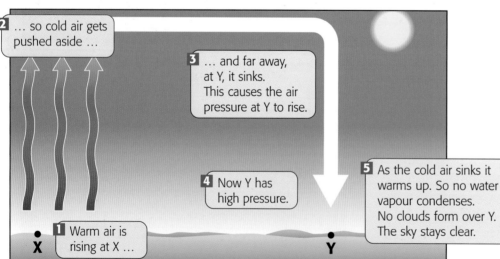

2 … so cold air gets pushed aside …

3 … and far away, at Y, it sinks. This causes the air pressure at Y to rise.

4 Now Y has high pressure.

5 As the cold air sinks it warms up. So no water vapour condenses. No clouds form over Y. The sky stays clear.

1 Warm air is rising at X …

X

Y

So high pressure means clear skies, with no clouds. And that gives our hottest summer weather, and coldest winter weather, as you'll see next.

▲ *To see if the air pressure is rising or falling, tap on a barometer.*

When there's high pressure in summer …

There are no clouds in the way so the sun is strong. Take care you don't get burned!

Since there is no cloud to trap the heat in, the evenings can be cool.

No cloud means no rain. So there may be **drought** in some places.

No cloud also means the ground gets cold at night. Water vapour condenses on grass to form **dew**.

But inland, on very hot cloudless days, the hot air may rise rapidly. It cools, and huge black clouds appear.

Inside these clouds, strong currents of air whip around, causing **thunderstorms** …

… and thunderstorms can lead to heavy rain and even **flooding**.

When there's high pressure in winter …

There is no cloud to act as a blanket. So the days are clear, cold and bright.

With no cloud, the ground cools fast at night, and cools the air above it. Water vapour condenses and freezes on cold surfaces, giving **frost**.

It also condenses on dust and other particles in the air, giving **fog**. This makes driving dangerous.

Pipes may burst and homes may get flooded.

Water on roads freezes into ice as the sun goes down.

Ice and frost mean animals have trouble finding food.

Your turn

1 Write this out, using the correct word from each pair.

Low pressure is a sign of fine/unsettled weather. The lower the pressure the calmer/stormier the weather will be. High pressure brings clear/cloudy skies, which means very hot/cold weather in summer and very warm/cold weather in winter.

2 For some jobs, long spells of high pressure weather can bring problems. Try to give three examples.

3 For some jobs, long spells of low pressure weather can bring problems. Write down three examples.

4 It's August, and high pressure. You're going camping. List four items you'll pack, to cope with the weather.

5 a What do fog, dew and frost have in common?
  b Explain how each forms.

6 Which type of weather do you prefer – high or low pressure? And in which season? Give your reasons.

Why is our weather so changeable?

Here you will learn why our weather can change so quickly.

Our changeable weather

The sun is shining. The sky is blue. Tomorrow is Sports Day. Everyone is excited.

And then tomorrow arrives. Heavy clouds, gusty winds, non-stop rain – and Sports Day spoiled.

So *why* does our weather change like this – and so fast? It's because of huge blocks of air on the move.

▲ *Another event spoiled by rain.*

Air on the move

Some parts of the Earth are hot. Some are cold. This causes the air to move around – like the air in a cold room when you turn on a heater.

Warm air always moves from a warmer place to a colder one. This pushes the colder air back towards the warmer place. It happens all around the Earth. Look at the simplified model on the right.

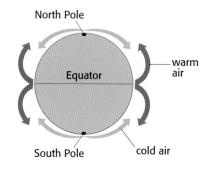

Air masses

The air moves in huge blocks called **air masses**. An air mass can be warm or cold, damp or dry, depending on where it came from.

An air mass coming from the North Pole will be cold and dry …

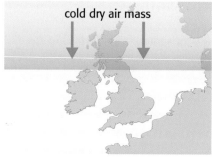

… so if it moves over the UK you'll get cold dry weather.

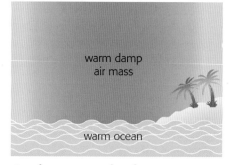

An air mass coming from a warm ocean will be warm and damp …

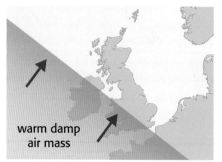

… and if it moves over the UK you get warm dampish weather.

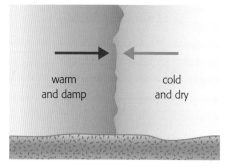

Often, two different air masses will meet and clash …

… and this causes sudden changes in the weather!

Air masses and us

The UK is nearly half way between the cold north pole and the hot equator. So it is in the path of many different air masses, that may meet and clash. This is the main reason our weather can change so fast.

How an air mass changes the weather

An air mass can bring wind, rain, and a change in temperature. Like this:

There's a cold air mass in your area.

So the morning is cool. And there is high pressure, so the sky is clear.

But a warm air mass is on the way. How will it affect the weather?

The warm air mass has arrived.
1 Warm air is lighter. So the warm air slides up over the cold air.
2 As it rises, the pressure falls. So the weather gets a bit windy.
3 As the rising air cools, a bank of cloud forms.
4 It starts to rain. It may rain for hours.

It's a few hours later. Now the cold air mass has moved on. The warm air mass has taken over.

So the afternoon feels warmer. The rain has eased off. The wind has dropped.

If there's a warm air mass in place, and a cold one arrives, you get even worse weather. Because a cold air mass travels fast. It dives under the warm one. So the air pressure rises sharply, giving strong gusty winds. The warm air is shoved upwards, giving thick cloud and heavy rain.

Fronts

The leading edge of an air mass is called a front.

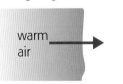

A **warm front** means a warm air mass is arriving.

A warm front is shown on a weather map like this.

A **cold front** means a cold air mass is arriving.

It's shown on a weather map like this.

Your turn

1 What is an air mass?

2 Five main types of air mass cross Britain. This map shows where they come from. (See page 141 too.)
Answer these questions by giving the labels A – E:
a Which air mass do you think is coldest, and dry? Why?
b Which two are dampest? Why?
c Which one is very cold and dry in winter, but warmer in summer? Try to explain why.
d Which one is warm even in winter?

3 It is 7 am on 16 March. There is a cold air mass in your area. A warm front will arrive about 4 pm. Write a weather forecast for the day, for your local radio.

4 What is: a a warm front? b a cold front?
Draw symbols for them. Beside each symbol write *warmer* and *colder* where you think they should go.

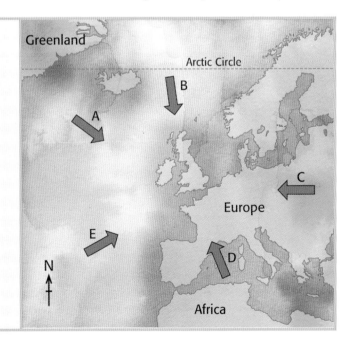

Storm!

From time to time, we get severe storms in the UK. Here you can read about one, and find out what caused it.

Stormy winds batter Britain

On the evening of Wednesday 17 January 2007, a storm swept into Britain from the Atlantic Ocean. It brought raging winds – up to 150 km an hour in some places – and torrential rain.

By Thursday afternoon, it had caused eleven deaths.

Three men were killed by falling trees. A little boy, and a woman, were crushed when walls fell on them. Two lorry drivers died when high winds pushed their lorries over. A third died when his lorry hit a car. A collapsing shed killed one man. Another was struck by a petrol station canopy. And one man died when the wind slammed him into a metal shutter.

All around the country, trees were uprooted and cars turned over. More than 130 000 homes were left without electricity, when power lines got blown down.

The storm brought travel chaos too. Many flights were cancelled. Roads were closed because of fallen trees, and flooding. Fallen trees and branches, and power lines, disrupted rail services.

The storm travels on

Then, leaving £350 million of damage behind, the storm crossed the North Sea. On the afternoon of 18 January, it had hit mainland Europe, heading for Poland and Russia. By the evening of 19 January, millions more homes were left without power, and 36 more people were dead.

From newspaper reports, January 2007

▲ *The winds blew down big trees.*

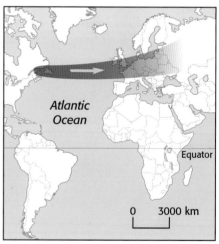

▲ *The path of the storm.*

◀ *Along our coast, the waves were whipped into a frenzy.*

What caused the storm?

Like most storms in the UK, that one was caused by a weather system called a **depression**. (Or sometimes it is called a **low**.)

A depression consists of a cold air mass chasing a warm one. The cold front dives quickly under the warm air mass, and shoves it upwards. The sudden big change in pressure gives rise to strong winds.

This diagram shows a cross-section (a side view) through a depression. Follow the numbers to see what happens.

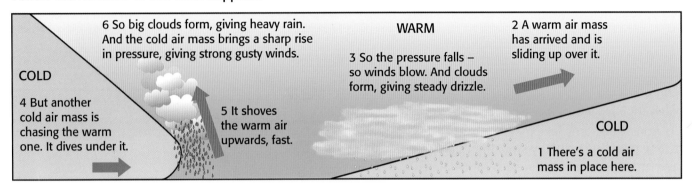

COLD

6 So big clouds form, giving heavy rain. And the cold air mass brings a sharp rise in pressure, giving strong gusty winds.

4 But another cold air mass is chasing the warm one. It dives under it.

5 It shoves the warm air upwards, fast.

WARM

3 So the pressure falls – so winds blow. And clouds form, giving steady drizzle.

2 A warm air mass has arrived and is sliding up over it.

COLD

1 There's a cold air mass in place here.

The depression dies away when all of the warm air mass has been lifted off the ground. As it rises, it cools to the same temperature as the cold air mass, so the two air masses blend together.

A weather chart for the storm

Look at this weather chart. It shows part of the depression, on 18 January, after it crossed the UK. The fronts are marked in.

The cold front brought a very big, sudden, rise in pressure. That's why the winds were so strong.

Look where part of the cold front has caught up with the warm one. It lifts it right off the ground. We call this an **occluded** front. The winds are at their most violent here.

In fact a depression acts like a giant whisk, mixing warm and cold air masses. And, as you saw, the result can be deadly.

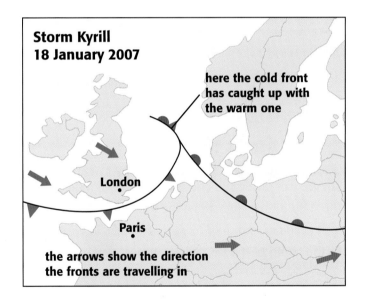

**Storm Kyrill
18 January 2007**

here the cold front has caught up with the warm one

London

Paris

the arrows show the direction the fronts are travelling in

Your turn

1 The storm was caused by a depression. What's a depression?

2 Look at the map on page 44. (Page 141 will help too.)
   a Where did the storm start?
   b Name eight European countries it passed through.
   c Where did it die out?
   d About how many km did it travel altogether?

3 Look at the top picture on page 44. The wind caused this damage. But what caused the wind?

4 It is 17 January 2007. You have to advise people how to stay safe, during the storm. What will you say? The report and photos on page 44 will give you clues.

5 Look where London and Paris are, on the map above. Which was warmer, at this point? Explain your answer.

6 It is the evening of 18 January, 2007. The storm will hit Poland in a couple of hours. Write a weather forecast for Polish TV.

7 Now explain what a depression is, as if to a 9-year-old.

From weather to climate

In this unit you will learn what climate is, and how to draw a climate graph.

Weather: a reminder

Weather is the state of the atmosphere at a given time.

The weather in Plymouth was good when this photo was taken. But it may have rained later. Because weather can change from hour to hour and day to day. Not like climate!

So what is climate?

Climate is the *average* weather in a place. It tells you what the weather is usually like, in any given month.

To work it out, they take measurements every day, over a long period (25 or 30 years). Then they calculate the average measurements for each month. Look at this table for Plymouth:

▲ A nice day in Plymouth – but what's the climate like there?

Plymouth

Climate data for Plymouth												
Average values	Jan	Feb	Mar	Apr	May	Jun	Jul	Aug	Sep	Oct	Nov	Dec
Temperature (°C)	8	8	10	12	15	18	20	19	18	15	11	10
Rainfall (mm)	99	74	69	53	63	53	70	77	78	91	113	110
Hours of sunshine/day	1.8	2.9	4.0	6.0	7.0	7.3	6.7	6.5	5.2	3.4	2.7	1.6
Number of days with gales	3.4	1.9	1.5	0.5	0.3	0.1	0	0.3	0.9	1.3	2.2	3

So the average temperature for July in Plymouth is 20 °C. For December it is 10 °C. And November is the wettest month.

Climate across the UK

Climate varies across the UK. (See why in the next unit.) But we can divide the country into four climate zones.

The map on the right show the four zones. Note that:

◆ it is colder and drier towards the east, in winter
◆ the south of the UK is the warmest part.

▲ Meteorologists work out climate data.

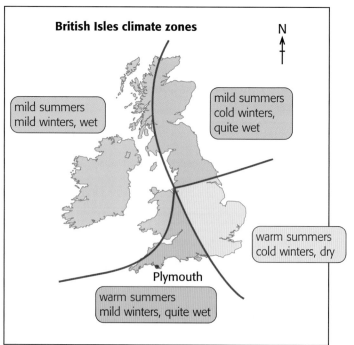

British Isles climate zones

N

mild summers
mild winters, wet

mild summers
cold winters,
quite wet

warm summers
cold winters, dry

Plymouth

warm summers
mild winters, quite wet

Your turn

1 What is: **a** weather? **b** climate?

2 Look at each statement **A–H** below and say whether it describes weather or climate.

   A It was a hot day in Boscombe when the photo on the right was taken.

   B November is usually the wettest month in Plymouth.

   C Egypt is usually very hot in August.

   D It rained heavily all afternoon.

   E May to September is the monsoon season, in South East Asia.

   F In September a terrible storm carried Richard's garden shed away.

   G There was heavy fog on the motorway last night. Visibility was less than a metre.

   H January is a good time to head for Florida, to catch some winter sun.

3 Look at the table for Plymouth, on page 46.

   a Which month usually has least sunshine?

   b Which month usually gets most gales?

   c Which month is usually warmest?

   d Which month do *you* think would be best for a camping holiday around Plymouth? Why?

   e Which do you think would be worst? Why?

4 Now look at this graph. It is a **climate graph** for London. It shows a bar chart and line graph together.

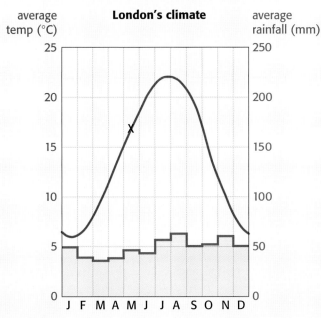

average temp (°C) — London's climate — average rainfall (mm)

   a What does the bar chart show? (Look on the blue axis.)

   b What does the line graph show? (The red axis.)

   c Which two months are usually hottest in London?

   d Which month is usually driest?

   e Which gets most rain? Can you explain why?

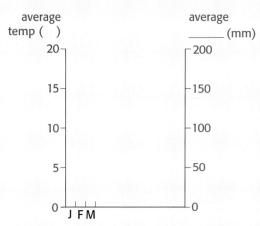

▲ *Boscombe in Dorset, basking in the sun.*

5 It's your turn to draw a climate graph – for Plymouth. You will use the data from the table on page 46.

   a Make a large copy of the axes shown below, and complete the labels. (Use graph paper if you can, and label each axis in a different colour.)

average temp ( ) — average _____ (mm)

   b Now draw in a bar chart showing rainfall for Plymouth. Check the bar chart for London, to see how to do it.

   c Next draw in a line graph for the temperature. Mark each point at the centre of the month (like the X for May, for London). Join the points with a smooth curve.

   d Give your graph a title.

6 Compare the climate graphs for London and Plymouth. Which of the two places:

   a gets more rain?   **b** is hotter in summer?

   c is colder in winter?

See if you can come up with a reason for each answer.

The factors that influence climate

In this unit you will learn why climate can be so different, in different places.

First, a reminder

In Unit 3.2, you saw that the sun, and water vapour, are the two main *causes* of weather. But many other factors *influence* the weather. Which means they influence the climate too.

Different places, different climates

Climate is what the weather is *usually* like in a place, in a given month. It can be very different in different places, and in different months. Look at this data:

Place	Month	Average temp (°C)	Average rainfall (mm)
Giza, Egypt	August	29	0
London, UK	August	17	51
London, UK	December	5	60

▲ *Giza, Egypt – where the pyramids are.*

The factors that influence climate

Why can climate be so different in different places, and different months? Let's look at the factors that influence it.

1 Latitude – the main factor

Latitude means how far a place is from the equator. The further away, the cooler it is. That's because the Earth is curved.

Look at A. These rays heat an area around the equator. It gets hot.

Now look at B. These rays give the same amount of heat. But the curve means they have to heat a larger area. So it gets less hot.

C heats an even larger area – so it hardly even gets warm!

So that is why:

◆ the UK is always cooler than Egypt.
◆ the north of the UK is usually cooler than the south.
◆ it is very cold at the North and South Poles.

2 The Earth's tilt

The Earth travels non-stop around the sun. It is tilted as it travels, as this diagram shows.

And that's why the climate in a place can be so different, in different months. The tilt gives our **seasons**.

Look at the diagram.

In June, the **northern hemisphere** – the top half of the Earth, where we live – is tilted towards the sun. So we have summer.

But by December, it is tilted away from the sun. So we get less heat. We have winter!

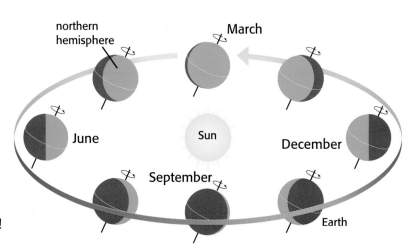

3 Other factors

Here are four other factors that affect the climate in a place.

Distance from the coast
The sea is cooler than land in summer, and warmer in winter. So a sea breeze keeps the coast cool in summer – and warm in winter!

Prevailing wind direction
For example in the UK the prevailing wind is from the south west. It brings water vapour from the ocean – and that means rain!

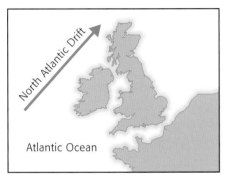

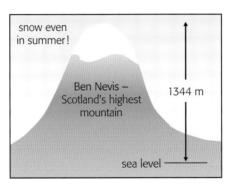

Ocean currents
For example a warm ocean current called the **North Atlantic Drift** warms the west coast of the UK in winter, by warming the wind.

Height above sea level
Or **altitude**. The higher you are above sea level, the cooler it is. The temperature falls by about 1 °C for every 100 metres.

▲ *Mt Kilimanjaro is in the hot tropics, in Africa. But it has snow on top!*

But the climate is changing …

Now the scary bit. Our climate is changing! The Earth is getting warmer.

Some scientists say this is due to changes in the sun, or wobbles in the Earth's path around the sun. But many say it's mainly because we humans burn so much fuel. Find out more in Chapter 5.

Your turn

1 Draw a spider map to show the factors that influence climate. Make it look interesting. (Add little drawings?)

2 Using the map on page 139, give *two* reasons why:
   a Aberdeen is colder than Plymouth in winter
   b It's colder up Ben Nevis than in Plymouth
   c London is warmer than Belfast in summer.

3 With the help of the world map on pages 140 – 141, explain why Tehran is hotter than Lisbon, in summer.

4 From the same world map, choose the capital city you think might be hottest in July. Explain your choice.

5 In the UK, the *prevailing wind* is a south west wind.
   a What does this mean? (Glossary!)
   b Explain how this wind affects the climate.
   c How would a prevailing *north* wind affect the climate?

6 A big challenge! See if you can explain why it gets colder as you go up a mountain.

Climates around the world

Did you know?
♦ Deserts are places with less than 25 cm of rain a year.
♦ Some deserts are hot, some cold.

Here you will see how climate varies around the world, and then give reasons why.

A world climate map

We can divide the Earth into different **climate regions**. Check out the key.

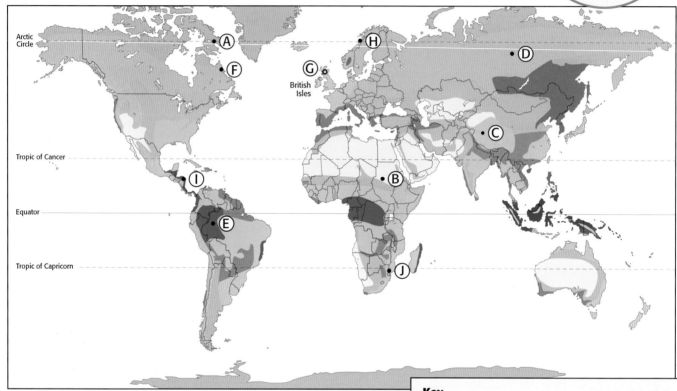

The different climates are due to the factors you met in Unit 3.9.

Look at the dark green region along the equator. The key shows that this region is hot and wet all year.

It is hot because the sun's rays are strongest at the equator. And wet because the hot air rises fast, its water vapour condenses to form thick clouds – and the rain pours down.

Now look at the place marked **A** on the map. What is the climate like here? Can you explain why?

The climate varies within regions

The map shows that the British Isles are in a region of warm summers, mild winters, and rain all year.

This does not mean that every part of the British Isles has the same climate. Some parts are warmer and drier, as you saw on page 46. But *overall*, the climate in the British Isles is quite mild, and quite damp.

What about 50 years from now?

50 years from now, a world climate map could look quite different, since the Earth is getting warmer. Places that are now very dry could become very wet, and vice versa. Find out more in Chapter 5.

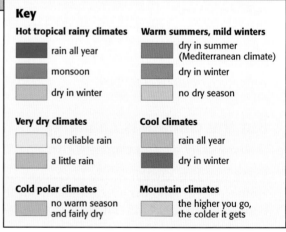

Key

Hot tropical rainy climates
- rain all year
- monsoon
- dry in winter

Very dry climates
- no reliable rain
- a little rain

Cold polar climates
- no warm season and fairly dry

Warm summers, mild winters
- dry in summer (Mediterranean climate)
- dry in winter
- no dry season

Cool climates
- rain all year
- dry in winter

Mountain climates
- the higher you go, the colder it gets

Did you know?
♦ The upper side of clouds reflects sunlight away, before it can reach the Earth.
♦ So clouds have a cooling effect during the day.

Your turn

1 Look at the map on page 50. What's the climate like at:
   a B?   b D?   c E?

2 Look again at the map. It is a lot cooler at **D** than at **B**. Suggest a reason.

3 Which of the climates on the map would *you*:
   a most like to live in? Why?
   b least like to live in? Why?

4 Now look at the map below. It shows the world's main mountain ranges, and *some* winds and ocean currents.
   a What are *ocean currents*? (Glossary?)
   b There is a warm current to the west of the UK. It is called …? (Unit 3.9.)
   c i Name a country that may be affected by a cold current. The map on pages 140 – 141 will help.
     ii In what way might the current affect it?
   d Now name a country where the prevailing wind is:
     i from the south east   ii from the north west

5 Below are some facts about places marked on the map on page 50. See if you can explain them. The map below, and what you learned in Unit 3.9, will help.
   a It is cold all year round at **C**.
   b **G** is at the same latitude as **F**, but is warmer.
   c **A** is at the same latitude as **H**, but is colder.
   d It is much hotter and drier at **B** than at **H**.
   e It is drier at **B** than at **I**, and hotter in the daytime.

6 Now look at this graph. It is a **climate graph** for a place called Frobisher Bay. The blue numbers and bars show rainfall. The red numbers and red line show temperature.

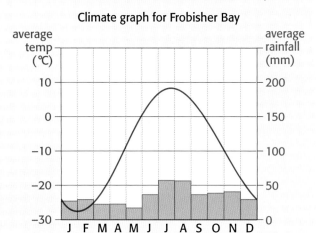

Climate graph for Frobisher Bay

Try these questions about the climate in Frobisher Bay.
   a Which two months are usually the wettest?
   b Which month is driest?
   c What is the average rainfall in August?
   d Which month is warmest?
   e For how many months of the year is it freezing?

7 Frobisher Bay is shown by a letter on the map on page 50. Which of these letters is it: **A**, **B**, **G** or **J**?

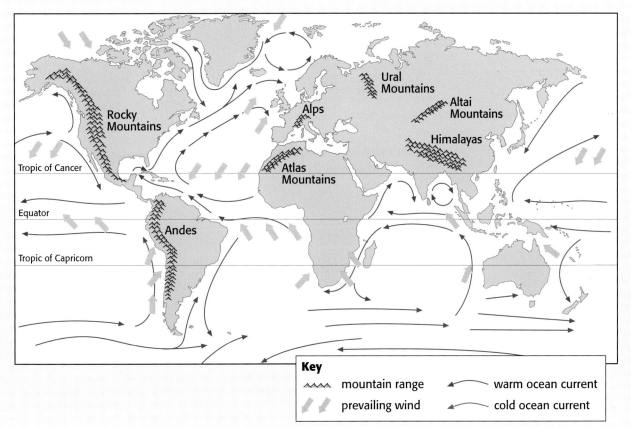

Key

⋀⋀⋀⋀ mountain range   ← warm ocean current

⇘⇘ prevailing wind   ← cold ocean current

4 Ecosystems

The big picture

This chapter is about **ecosystems**. These are the big ideas behind the chapter:

◆ An ecosystem is made up of plants and animals, and their non-living environment (air, water, soil, climate, and so on).

◆ The Earth can be divided up into large ecosystems, each with its own kinds of plants and animals.

◆ Climate is the key factor that makes these ecosystems so different.

◆ Ecosystems are fragile. So we must watch out, or we'll destroy them.

Your goals for this chapter

By the end of this chapter you should be able to answer these questions:

◆ What do these terms mean?
vegetation   ecosystem   biome   decomposer   nutrient

◆ Where on the Earth is the rainforest ecosystem, and what is its climate like?

◆ In what ways have plants adapted to living in the rainforests? (Give four examples.)

◆ How and why are we humans destroying the rainforests?

◆ What is the link between rainforests and global warming?

◆ Where on the Earth is the tundra ecosystem, and what is its climate like?

◆ In what ways have plants and animals adapted to living in the tundra? (Give three examples for each.)

◆ The tundra ecosystem is under threat. What threats does it face? And which one will affect us all?

And then ...

When you finish the chapter, come back to this page and see if you have met your goals!

Did you know?
◆ Today the Earth is losing species of plants and animals very fast.
◆ Scientists call it mass extinction.

Did you know?
◆ There are over 5000 different kinds of frog.
◆ The smallest is just 1 cm long!

Did you know?
◆ An area of rainforest the size of a football field is destroyed every second!

What if...
◆ ... you had a rainforest to look after?

What if...
◆ ... ecosystems found a way to destroy humans?

Your chapter starter

Look at the photo on page 52. What is that creature?

Do you think you'd find one like it, near you?

Can you think of a way its colour may help it?

How might those big eyes help it? And those big feet?

Name some animals that do live wild, near you.

How did YOU get in here?

Climate and ecosystems

In this unit you will learn what ecosystems are, and how they relate to climate.

Climate regions

The Earth can be divided into regions with different climates.
Page 50 has a map of them.
And these photos are from four of them.

This is a **hot desert**, in the hot dry climate region. What do you notice about the vegetation (plants)? What is that strange animal?

Does this look familiar? It is **deciduous forest,** in the climate region with warm summers, mild winters, and rain all year. That's the region we live in.

Hot desert

Deciduous forest

Key
- hot desert
- Arctic tundra
- tropical rainforest
- deciduous forest

Equator

Where they are found

Tropical rainforest

Tundra

Tropical rainforests are found in the hot wet climate region – where it is hot and wet all year. Animals such as monkeys and parrots live here.

This shows **tundra**, in the cold dry polar climate region. The soil below the surface is always frozen. What animal is that?

They are all ecosystems

The photos on page 54 show four different **ecosystems**.
An ecosystem is a natural unit made up of:

◆ living things (plants and animals) and
◆ the surroundings or **environment** they live in – the air, water, soil, and the climate (how warm or wet it is).

A pond is a tiny ecosystem. A tropical rainforest is a large one.

There are tropical rainforests in over 80 countries. Together, they make up a very large ecosystem. All the hot deserts make up another, and so on. These very large ecosytems are often called **biomes**.

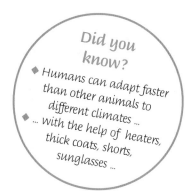

Did you know?
◆ *Humans can adapt faster than other animals to different climates ...*
◆ *... with the help of heaters, thick coats, shorts, sunglasses ...*

Why are they so different?

The ecosystems in the photos all are very different – because of the climate.
Look at this diagram:

The climate
Climate is the driving force in an ecosystem.
The climate affects …

So everything in an ecosystem is linked. The plants and animals depend on each other – and on the environment.

1 **the soil**
How thick and rich the soil is depends partly on the climate. Rock breaks down fast into soil in a hot damp climate.

which influences …

2 **the vegetation (plants and trees)**
It **adapts** to suit the climate and soil. It grows fast and thick in a hot damp sunny climate, and slowly in a cold dry one.

which influences …

3 **the animals**
They **adapt** to cope with the climate, and to feed on the plants, or each other.

You can find out more about two of those ecosystems – tropical rainforests, and tundra – in the rest of this chapter.

Your turn

1 Choose one photo from page 54. Imagine you are there. What's it like? You can answer like this:

> I can see …
> I can hear …
> I can smell …
> I feel …
> I would like …

2 Explain what this term means. (Glossary?)
   a ecosystem   b environment   c adapt   d biome
3 Look at these two climate graphs. They match two of the ecosystems on page 54.
   a One is for the deciduous forest ecosystem. Which one?
   b Which ecosystem does the other graph match?

4 The living things in an ecosystem depend on each other, and on the environment. See if you can give an example. (One student thought of squirrels/ trees/ soil.)

Climate graph A
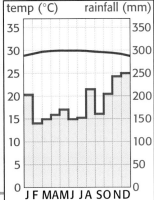

Climate graph B
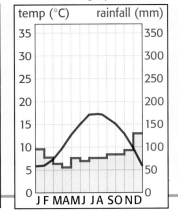

The tropical rainforests

Here you'll see how the rainforests grew, and adapted to a hot wet climate.

The Earth's richest ecosystem

Vegetation grows well in hot damp places – like tropical rainforests! There you'll find thousands of species of trees and plants. And thousands of species of insects and other animals, that live in them.

The vegetation

Four layers

The trees and plants of the rainforest form four layers:

1 the emergents
These are the tallest trees, up to 60 m tall.

2 the canopy
It's the thickest layer, where most of the animals live.

3 the under-canopy
It has young trees, shorter trees, and bushes.

4 the shrub layer
Here you find ferns and other plants that grow close to the ground.

Adaptations

The vegetation has adapted to get sunlight, and protect itself. Look at these examples.

A The **emergents** reach sunlight by growing tall.

B Thick vines called **lianas** reach sunlight by looping around tree branches.

C Plants called **epiphytes** just perch on high branches. They feed on rain, and nutrients from rotting leaves.

D Here in the shady shrub layer, plants grow large leaves with lots of chlorophyll, to trap as much sunlight as possible.

E The tallest trees have big strong **buttress roots**, to stop themselves falling over.

F Roots don't grow deep into the soil. They spread out near the surface.

This way, they can quickly take up the nutrients from dead leaves and animal droppings. (These nutrients are released by the worms and other decomposers.)

The soil

The soil is deep. But only the top few inches are much good. Here's why.

When dead leaves and animal droppings fall to the forest floor, they are quickly broken down by insects, worms and bacteria (**decomposers**).

This releases **nutrients**. These are quickly taken up by plant and tree roots, before they can soak deep into the soil.

G And look at some ways the leaves protect themselves:

sharp edges keep hungry things away

thick waxy coat protects against rain and insects

drip tip lets rain drip off

The animals

Millions of different kinds of animals live in the rainforest. Here are just three:

The emerald tree boa. It can grow over 2 m long. At night, it hangs from a branch to catch its prey: rodents, lizards, and small birds.

The sloth. Its strong claws allow it to hang from branches. Its hair is filled with green algae (tiny plants) to help it hide among the leaves.

The toucan. This bird lives high in the canopy. Its beak helps it feed on fruit, seeds, and berries. It has a loud call, that scares enemies.

Biodiverse

The rainforests are our most biodiverse ecosystem – they have the biggest variety of living things. They cover less than 7% of the Earth's land, but hold over half the known species of plants and animals. They're jumping!

Did you know?
◆ Insects are classed as animals.

Full of treasures

Rainforests gave us fruits like bananas and pineapples. And *thousands* of medical drugs. Aspirin is a copy of a chemical from a rainforest plant. Many cancer drugs come from rainforest plants. Scientists have studied only a tiny % of rainforest plants, so far. They hope to find many other useful drugs.

Your turn

1 What do you think is the best thing about rainforests?
2 Copy and complete. The glossary may help for some.
  a The emergents are …
  b Many leaves have drip tips so that …
  c Nutrients are substances that …
  d Roots grow close to the soil surface so that …
  e The emergents have buttress roots so that …
  f The plants on the forest floor have dark green leaves all year round so that …
  g Decomposers are …
  h Most insects and animals in the rainforest live in the canopy, because …
3 The drawing on the right shows part of a rainforest.
  a Make a large copy of it. Then copy each sentence from below the drawing into the correct box.
  b When the trees are cut down, the soil soon becomes useless. See if you can explain why.
4 Do you agree with this person? Explain.

Rainforests? Nothing to do with me!

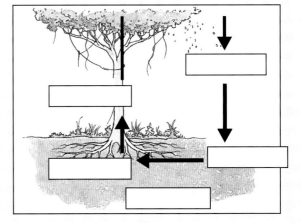

The roots quickly take up the nutrients again.

Decomposers release the nutrients from them.

The nutrients help the vegetation to grow.

Dead leaves and animal waste fall all year round.

The soil down here is poor because the nutrients don't get a chance to sink in.

e doing to the rainforests?

ECOSYSTEMS

... destroying the tropical rainforests.

...?

... the tropics. (Easy!)
... tropical rainforest. But just 10
...: nearly 80% between them.

...ppening to them?

For thousands of years, the rainforests were barely disturbed. The humans that lived in them gathered fruit, and fished, and hunted wild animals. But they did not harm the forests.

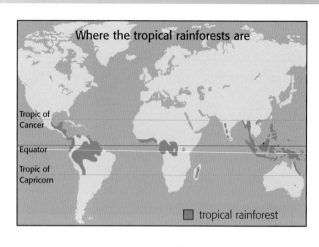

Where the tropical rainforests are

Tropic of Cancer

Equator

Tropic of Capricorn

☐ tropical rainforest

Now we are destroying them fast. In ways like these:

Large areas are being burned, to clear land for farming. Some by poor farmers, to grow food …

… and some by big companies, to set up cattle ranches, or oil palm plantations, to make money.

Logging companies are big culprits. They cut down trees for timber, for things like furniture and doors.

About half the Earth's tropical rainforest has now gone – about 8 million square km. That's an area nearly the size of the USA. Much of it went in the last 50 years. And what's left is in danger.

Read on, to find out about the rainforest in Indonesia.

Indonesia's rainforest at risk

Look at this photo. Great furniture. Soon, when the guests arrive, great food will be served. And it's another little nibble from Indonesia's rainforest.

Logging is rampant in the rainforest there. Some has a licence from the government. But much is illegal. The wood is used for things like furniture, and doors, and windows. Some finds its way to the UK.

The loggers target just the trees they want. But when a huge mahogany or maranti tree is cut down, several others crash down with it.

Logging is not the only link with the photo.

Rainforest is also being cleared to make way for oil palm trees. Their fruit gives palm oil – and we can't get enough of that. It is used as cooking oil, and in bread, cakes, chocolate, candles, soap, and detergents, for a start.

Now palm oil has another use: as a biofuel. It is being added to diesel, in diesel engines… to help in the fight against global warming.

▲ Once it was rainforest, full of different plants and animals. Now it's an oil palm plantation.

▲ You'll find orangutan in the rainforest on two Indonesian islands. And nowhere else in the world! So they are in danger.

Your turn

1 The map on page 58 shows where the rainforests are.
  a It is hot in those places. Why? (Page 48?)
  b It rains heavily in the afternoons, in the rainforests. See if you can work out why. (Page 38 may help.)
  c Europe has no tropical rainforests. Why not?

2 The top 10 rainforest countries are: Brazil, the Democratic Republic of Congo, Indonesia, Peru, Bolivia, Angola, Venezuela, Papua New Guinea, Mexico, India.
  a Make a table with headings like this:

The top 10 rainforest countries	
Country	Continent

  b Then fill in the countries and their continents. See how many you can do *without* looking at the map on pages 140–141.

3 The bar graph on the right shows how fast the rainforest is being destroyed.
  a Which continent is losing its rainforest fastest?
  b What overall trend does the graph show?

4 There may be a link between the crisps you buy, and rainforest loss. See if you can draw a strip cartoon like the one started here, to show it. (Up to 7 boxes okay.)

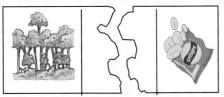

5 Now find Indonesia on the map on pages 140–141. (It's near Australia.) Give five geographical facts about it, using the map to help you.

6 These are opinions from four Indonesians. Choose at least two of them, and write replies.

a Why worry? They are just trees. It doesn't matter if we cut them down.

b You buy our wood and palm oil. And then you blame us for cutting down the rainforest. Hypocrites!

c Indonesia is quite poor. We need to make money from our rainforest if we can.

d You have cut down most of the forests in your own country. Why stop us?

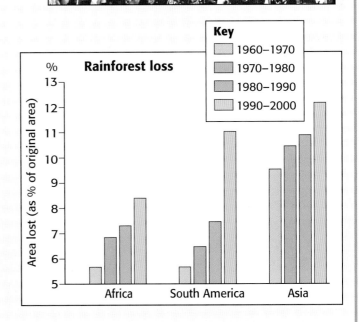

Key
- 1960–1970
- 1970–1980
- 1980–1990
- 1990–2000

Rainforest loss

Area lost (as % of original area)

Africa   South America   Asia

New hope for the rainforests?

Here you'll find out about a new scheme to save the tropical rainforests.

Protesting in vain

Some people have worried about the rainforests for years, and tried to save them. With little success, because …

The poor farmers deep in the rainforest, slashing and burning it, don't care. They need land to grow food for their hungry families.

The rainforest countries are mostly poor. They can earn money by selling things like timber and palm oil, to the rich countries.

And meanwhile, we in the rich countries keep on buying things that are linked to the destruction of the rainforest.

For example, Indonesia is quite poor. It owes 59 billion dollars to other countries. It wants to sell as much timber and palm oil as it can, to pay off its debts.

But now… global warming

The air all around the Earth is getting warmer. We call it **global warming**.

Most scientists blame carbon dioxide. This gas forms when we burn coal, oil, gas, wood, and anything else that contains carbon. Then it acts like a blanket around the Earth, keeping heat in.

Global warming is already causing more storms, and floods, and droughts. It will mean disaster for many people. (Find out more on page 73.)

▲ *For years, protests made no difference.*

What has it got to do with the rainforests?

Plenty!

Trees take in carbon dioxide from the air. It's the starting point for all the things they need, to grow.

But if they are burned, to clear the ground for farming or ranching, carbon dioxide is given out again.

And if they are chopped down, the stumps and roots rot. This process gives out carbon dioxide too.

So the rainforests are like a giant store of locked-up carbon.
Destroying them releases carbon dioxide.
That helps to speed up global warming. So we will all suffer.

A new approach to saving the rainforests

Now there's a new approach to saving the rainforests. Read on!

At last, a happy rainforest story

'It's brilliant' said the minister from the Indonesian government. 'We rainforest countries got together, and came up with a great plan.'

'We have been destroying our rainforests for years. Mostly because you rich countries want timber and stuff – and we need the money!'

'But with global warming, we will all suffer. Rich and poor. And they say cutting down the rainforests is making it worse.'

'So here's the deal. We will protect our rainforests from now on. But you rich countries must pay us to do it.'

'It's only fair. You cut down your own forests centuries ago, for wood for industry, and to make room for cities and farms. Now you want us to keep our rainforests, to slow down global warming. We will be happy to do it, sure. But you will have to pay.'

First payment agreed

In fact the first payment to Indonesia has been agreed already. The state of Aceh will receive $26 million, over five years, for protecting two million hectares of rainforest.

Most of the money will go to local villages, for things like schools, and health centres, and sustainable farming. But only if they can prove that trees are not being cut down.

So forest wardens, and satellites, will be watching.

From news reports, January 2008

▲ *You can record trees, using a GPS system…*

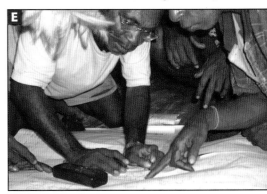
▲ *… then map them on a map.*

▼ *You can also use satellite images to keep an eye on logging.*

Your turn

1 What is *global warming*? Why is it bad news?

2 Copy and complete:
   a Carbon dioxide is …
   b Rainforests take in carbon dioxide for …
   c Rainforests give out carbon dioxide when …
   d The more carbon dioxide there is in the air …

3 You are the man in photo **A**. They offer you money to look after the rainforest, not cut it down. How do you feel about that? Tell us!

4 Satellite images can be used to guard the rainforest. **F** is a satellite image. It shows part of a rainforest. See if you can work out what these are:
   a the thick brown wavy line   b the dark green area
   c the lighter green area   d the other brown shapes
   e the white fluffy things

5 You live in Aceh, in Indonesia. You are in charge of protecting the rainforest. How will you do it? Photos **D**, **E** and **F** may give you ideas. Try to think of others too. Then write an action plan, as bullet points.

6 Oil palms grow fine on worn-out land. Farmers don't need to chop down rainforest.
   a Name your favourite sweets (or crisps, or biscuits, or soap, or shampoo).
   b They almost certainly contain palm oil. How would you feel if rainforest was cut down for it?
   c How could you check?

7 Suppose *all* the rainforest countries are paid to protect their rainforests. Name all the groups who will benefit. (Will animals benefit? Will you?)

The Arctic tundra

Here you will find out what, and where, the Arctic tundra ecosystem is – and how living things have adapted to living there.

What is the Arctic tundra?

The Arctic tundra is the ecosystem that lies up around the North Pole:

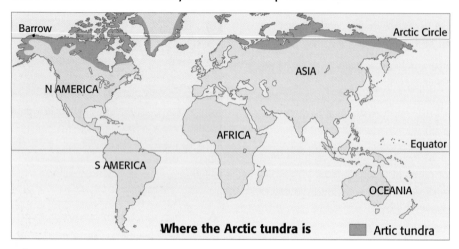

Where the Arctic tundra is | ▨ Artic tundra

▲ *A polar bear on the frozen tundra.*

What is it like there?

◆ Winters are long, cold and dark. The average temperature is around – 30 °C. By mid-December it is dark all day.

◆ Summers are very cool (3 to 12 °C) and short, but with long hours of daylight. By mid-July it is light for 24 hours a day.

◆ It is dry. There is less than 25 cm a year of rain or snow.

◆ There are harsh, biting winds.

◆ It is so cold that most of the soil is frozen hard all year. It is called **permafrost**. But the top layer thaws for 2 or 3 months every summer. Then plants grow quickly, covering it in a green carpet.

◆ There are no trees. Their roots can't grow down into the permafrost.

◆ When it does rain, or the top layer of soil thaws, the water can't soak away through the permafrost. So bogs, streams, and ponds appear in summer.

Plants of the tundra

The tundra is a harsh place. Even so, it is home to many species of plants and animals. (But not nearly as many as in the rainforests.)

Plants need warmth, and sunlight for **photosynthesis**. So how do they cope with the climate in the tundra? Like this:

◆ They have adapted to carry out photosynthesis at low temperatures, in low light – even when covered with snow!

◆ They grow low to the ground, and close together, for protection from the cold and wind.

◆ The growing season is short, so they grow fast. Some send out underground stems or **runners** that sprout new plants, instead of waiting to form flowers tund seeds.

▲ *The tundra in summer. Look at the ponds. These animals are reindeer (also called caribou).*

▲ *Some tundra flowers.*

Animals of the tundra

The animals of the tundra include:

◆ **carnivores** or meat-eating animals, such as brown bears and Arctic foxes

◆ **herbivores**, such as musk ox and reindeer (caribou), that feed on plants

◆ birds and insects.

Here are some ways animals have adapted to the harsh climate:

◆ Many have a thick outer coat of coarse waterproof fur, to keep them dry. And an inner coat of fluffy hair to trap heat.

◆ Many build up a thick layer of fat, ready for winter.

◆ Short legs, tails and snouts help to cut down heat loss.

◆ Some move in the winter. The birds fly south to warmer climates. Reindeer move to where they can find lichen, their winter food.

Look at these examples:

Tundra swans escape from the winter cold. Every year they fly up to 6000 km south, to warmer coastal areas in the USA.

The brown bear has a thick coat. It grows a thick layer of fat for winter. It digs a den and stays inside for the coldest months.

Musk oxen have thick shaggy coats, with fluffy hair underneath. Short legs help to reduce heat loss. They huddle for warmth and safety.

The Arctic fox has shorter legs, tail, ears and snout than British foxes, to reduce heat loss. Its thick coat goes white in winter, to help it hide.

Your turn

1 a Name five countries with tundra. (Pages 140 –141?)
   b Which country has the world's largest area of tundra?

2 This climate graph is for the town of Barrow, in the tundra in Alaska. (It is marked on the map on page 62.)
   a In which month does the top layer of soil start thawing?
   b Which months are the growing season for plants?
   c In which month are you likely to find most water in ponds and bogs? Explain.
   d In which month does all the permafrost thaw out?
   e In which months does *snow* fall?
   f Musk oxen dig under ice and snow for food, with their hooves. In which months do they need to do that?
   g Tundra swans leave the tundra in October, flying south. They are back again by mid-May. So what sort of temperatures are *too low* for the tundra swans?

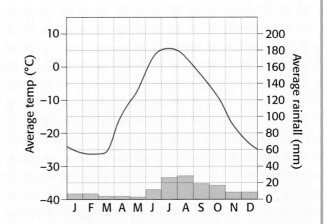

3 a So *why* is it so cold in the tundra?
   b Why does it stay bright 24 hours a day, in July?
   c Why does it stay dark 24 hours a day, in December?
   Unit 3.9 will help, if you get stuck.

Humans in the Arctic tundra

Here you'll learn about the people who live in the Arctic tundra, and what they do there.

Who lives there?

Bitter cold, biting winds, frozen ground, months of darkness. How could anyone live in the Arctic tundra? About 4 million people do!

There are two main groups of people:

◆ the **indigenous** people, whose ancestors have been there for thousands of years.

◆ descendants of people who arrived much later. (Lots of new people arrived in the last 30 or 40 years.)

The second group is about nine times larger than the first.

The indigenous people of the tundra

The first arrivals

The first people arrived in the tundra about 10 000 years ago. They were **hunter-gatherers**, like all our ancestors. There was plenty to hunt: woolly mammoth, reindeer, bears, musk ox, seal, walrus, and fish in the icy rivers. In the summers, they gathered berries and seeds.

They lived a **nomadic** life, always on the move. They lived in rough shelters. They dried meat and fish, to store for the winter. They wore animal skins and furs to keep warm.

Then, perhaps around 7000 years ago, they began to herd reindeer for meat and milk. They moved around with them, looking for pasture.

The indigenous people today

Today, about 400 000 descendants of those early settlers still live in the tundra. There are many different groups. (The list on the right gives some.) They all speak different languages.

▲ A Nenets girl with her two puppies, outside her chum (tent) in the Russian tundra. Her family herd reindeer. When the reindeer have eaten all the grass under the snow, the tent is packed up, and the family move on.

Some indigenous people of the tundra

◆ In Canada and the USA:
  Inuit
  Inuvialuit

◆ In Greenland:
  Inuit

◆ In Scandinavia:
  Sami

◆ In Russia:
  Nenets
  Enets
  Sami
  Selkups

Did you know?
◆ The indigenous people of the tundra find the term 'Eskimo' insulting.

◄ A reindeer herder in the Russian tundra. One herder may look after over a thousand reindeer. The reindeer will be sold to meat factories.

How their lives are changing

Life is changing for the indigenous people.

◆ Many still live by hunting and fishing. But instead of sleds and spears they now go by snowmobile, use guns and fishing rods – and live in houses.

◆ Some still live in tents, moving with their reindeer. But they send their children to boarding school, to make sure they get a good education.

◆ Many live in tundra towns and cities. They may find work in factories, or on oil fields, or on fishing boats. (They often find it hard to get other work, because they did not spend much time at school.)

The later arrivals

Here are some of the later arrivals:

◆ In the 17th and 18th century, fur traders and trappers arrived, and missionaries, and whalers, and people looking for gold.

◆ People moved in to 'run' the tundra for their governments.

◆ In the last 40 years or so, oil and mining companies have arrived, looking for oil, and gas, and metal ores. The tundra is rich in these – and it has not all been explored yet.

Settlements in the tundra

Most people live in scattered villages, towns, and small cities.

Some towns started as trading posts, set up by the fur traders. They swopped things like knives, kettles, and alcohol, for animal furs. Then they sold the furs for high prices, back home in Europe.

Some started as fishing centres.

But the largest settlements grew because of oil, and mining. Norilsk, in Russia, is one of the largest tundra cities. (Population 130 000.) It began over 70 years ago as a prison camp, for prisoners sent to work in the nickel mines. It is still a centre for mining and smelting metal ores – and one of the most polluted cities in the world.

▲ An Inuit mum picks up her children from school by snowmobile, in the Canadian tundra.

▲ Fumes from metal smelting in Norilsk, in the Russian tundra. This city is inside the Arctic circle.

Your turn

1 The Arctic tundra covers an area of about 12 million square kilometres. About 4 million people live in it.
 a Work out the population density there. (Glossary?)
 b The population density in the UK is 248 people per sq km. Write a short paragraph comparing the population densities in the UK and the tundra. Make it interesting!

2 a What does the term *indigenous people* mean?
 b Name one tribe of indigenous people of the tundra.
 c The indigenous people do not grow crops. Why not?

3 Look at the first photo on page 64. What do you think the family does for light, water, and heating?

4 Some things are much more difficult in the tundra than in the UK. See if you can say why this might be extra difficult:
 a disposing of sewage
 b building a new house
 c going to school in winter
 d mining
 e being a police detective

5 You have just been offered a new job: working for a newspaper, in the Canadian tundra. The pay is good. Write an e-mail to your cousin, telling her about the job offer, and why you will / won't accept it.

Tundra under threat

The tundra ecosystem is in danger. Here you'll find out why.

Under threat – from what?

The Arctic tundra is a harsh, frozen place. But it is also fragile. The ecosystem is in danger, thanks to …

♦ hunting
♦ extraction of oil, gas, and metal ores
♦ and, last but not least, global warming.

Hunting

Hundreds of years ago, hunters hunted just for the food they needed. But as the trade in fur and skins grew, more and more animals were hunted for these too. Some were hunted to danger levels.

Today, some tourists travel to the tundra to hunt, for sport. Small planes fly them to remote places.

At the same time, fishing boats trawl the seas off the coast, scooping up the fish that seals, polar bears, and other animals depend on.

Many species are now at risk, because their numbers have fallen so low. They include wolves, musk oxen, polar bears, grizzly bears, seals, sealions and walruses. So they are protected by law. You may be allowed to hunt some – but only if you buy a permit.

Extraction of oil, gas, and metal ores

The tundra is rich in oil, gas, and metal ores. And companies are keen to get their hands on them.

In Alaska, USA

Oil is big business in Alaska, USA. The oil fields are in the tundra. The oil is carried off by a pipeline called the Trans-Alaska pipeline. It is 1300 km long, and runs across the tundra to an ice-free port. (Look for Alaska on the map on page 140.)

Because of the permafrost, much of the pipe is above ground. Where it's buried, it is insulated, to make sure it does cause the permafrost to melt.

Oil leaks from the pipeline from time to time. People worry about this. And they worry that drilling might start in the Arctic National Wildlife Refuge, in Alaska. This area has oil, but is protected from drilling for now.

In Russia

In the Russian tundra, reindeer pastures have been taken over for mining, and oil and gas production, and new towns to support these.

The air, land, and water are polluted by toxic waste from mining and smelting. That's bad for the people and animals.

New roads are built on a thick layer of gravel, up to 2 metres thick, to stop the permafrost from thawing. That makes it hard for the reindeer to move around. All this is causing conflict with the reindeer herders.

▲ A good shot?

▲ Part of the Trans-Alaska pipeline.

▲ The pale grey stuff is permafrost. It starts to thaw once it is exposed.

The biggest threat of all: global warming

As you saw on page 60, the air around the Earth is getting warmer. We call it **global warming**. And it could destroy the tundra.

Most scientists blame carbon dioxide, from all the fuels we burn. They call it a **greenhouse gas**, because it traps heat around the Earth.

The big thaw

'It's a crazy house', says Eva. 'Nothing straight. We tried propping it up but that didn't work. We're going to have to move out sometime soon.'

And indeed it does look crazy. The walls are tilted. Opening and closing doors is tricky. Put something in the cupboard, and it slides away.

Why? Because the permafrost under the house is thawing.

Scientists say much of the tundra permafrost will thaw, thanks to global warming. Homes, schools, hospitals, roads … all will be affected.

Melting ice at the coast

The ice along the coast is melting too. So animals like the polar bears, that eat fish, have to swim further for their food. And they have less ice to live and breed on. Their numbers will fall even further.

The news gets worse

The permafrost is packed with dead, deep-frozen vegetation. When it melts, the vegetation will rot. If it rots near the surface, where there is oxygen, vast amounts of carbon dioxide will be released.

But if it rots deep in soggy ground, where there is no oxygen, methane will form instead. And methane is a much more powerful greenhouse gas than carbon dioxide.

Either way, the result is the same. Global warming will speed up. And give even more storms, floods, drought, and famine, around the world.

From news reports, 2008

▲ *Built on top of the permafrost – and now the permafrost is thawing.*

▲ *Where has my ice gone?*

Your turn

1 Look at the first photo on page 66.
  a How do you think the man is feeling?
  b How do you feel about what he has done? Why?

2 Think about those three threats to the tundra. Then arrange them in order of importance, biggest threat first.

3 a Do you agree with this person? Say why.
  b Do you think they will stop? Give your reasons.

Stop oil and gas extraction in the tundra **NOW!!!**

4 When permafrost thaws:
  a some results are *local*. Try to give two examples.
  b some results are *global*. Explain.

5
If the permafrost thaws deep down, lakes and ponds will disappear. The tundra will become very dry. This will be a disaster for the reindeer herders.

  a Try to explain why lakes and ponds will disappear.
  b Why would the tundra then become a very dry place? (Check out page 62!)
  c Why would that be a disaster, for reindeer herders?

5 Our warming planet

The big picture

This chapter is about **global warming**. These are the big ideas behind the chapter:

◆ Temperatures around the world are rising. We call it global warming.

◆ Some scientists say it's just a natural change.

◆ But most say it's mainly due to carbon dioxide, the gas that forms when we burn fuels.

◆ Global warming will bring disasters such as drought, and famine, and floods.

◆ We can't stop global warming. But we must try to limit it, before it's too late.

Your goals for this chapter

By the end of this chapter you should be able to answer these questions:

◆ What do these terms mean?

global warming   climate change   emissions

◆ How may climate change affect our world?
(Give at least six predictions.)

◆ What are greenhouse gases, and which can I name? (At least three.)

◆ Carbon dioxide is the greenhouse gas that concerns us most. Why?
And where does it come from?

◆ When we burn fuels, we affect people in other countries. Why?

◆ What can I do, on my own, to help reduce carbon dioxide emissions?
(Give at least four things.)

◆ What could: i governments do ii scientists do
to reduce carbon dioxide emissions?
(Give at least two sensible things for each.)

And then …

When you finish this chapter, come back to this page and see if you have met your goals!

Did you know?
◆ There have been at least four Ice Ages in the Earth's past …
◆ … when much of the Earth was covered in really thick ice.

Did you know?
◆ If Greenland's ice sheet melts, sea levels around the world will rise by 7 metres.

Did you know?
◆ If the average global temperature rises by 4 °C from now, up to 70% of species may become extinct.

Your chapter starter

Look at the photo on page 68. It shows a man dressed as a bear.

What kind of bear?

Why is he dressed like this?

Why did he spell 'barely' that way?

He thinks there's barely any time left. What does he mean?

Can we go somewhere cooler?

Saturday 30 April, 2050

Our planet is getting warmer. So what will life be like in 2050?
This unit makes some guesses.

Molly, UK

Molly is sitting on the balcony, in her T-shirt and shorts.

It is a perfect morning. The sun is hot, and the sky a brilliant blue.
A huge red butterfly flaps by. 'That's new', she thinks. Lots of new
insects are appearing these days. Then she hears the familiar whine
of a mosquito. It's okay. She has her mozzie spray on already.

She looks out over the farm. The orange trees are a mass of white
blossom. Six months from now, she will help her dad pick the
oranges. They will pack them into crates, fill up the truck with
hydrogen, and head off to Reading, to sell them. She loves going
there. She might buy another T-shirt, if she can save up enough.
But clothes are *so* expensive.

She picks up her dad's diginews. Today's news floods the screen.
Egypt and Sudan still at war, over Nile water. Drought in California.
Tension in the Arctic. Floods in New York. Another big outbreak
of Ebola fever in London. Gruesome!

She puts it down again. It's all a bit depressing. She will listen to
music instead.

▲ *An orange orchard. Near Reading?*

Aban and Numa, Kenya

'Wake up, Numa', says Aban. He shakes his little sister. She looks so
sad, and tired, that he gives her a cuddle. And then the two of them
climb out of the field where they slept.

There is a long walk ahead. Maybe two or three days – he can't tell.
It is two days since they left home. They closed the door of the hut
and crept out of the village at dawn. They said goodbye to no one.
There was no point. The few people left would soon be dead, from
thirst and hunger.

He is lucky. He still has the two eggs he cooked in the ashes. And
the last wrinkled mango from the tree he had tried so hard to keep
alive. It's not much food – but better than nothing.

What will they do when they get to the coast? He is not sure.
But he knows they must leave the country. They will try to get to
Europe, somehow. He has heard that people there have plenty of
water and food.

And so they trudge along. Two small figures on a dusty red track,
lit up by the hot morning sun.

▲ *It's a long long way to the coast, for
Aban and Numa.*

Captain Hanna, the Arctic Ocean

Captain Hanna stands at the rail of the *Arctic Sunrise*.

On the deck below, the tourists are out strolling already, lunch over. Some sit on the benches, wrapped in their warm rugs, sipping their coffee.

They are still a few days from the North Pole. With winter nearly over, all the ice will have gone by now. So the tourists can get onto the floating platform. People just love standing there, right on top of the North Pole.

In the distance, he can see a warship. That's a worry. There is so much talk about war, these days. Canada, Russia, Norway, America: all claiming the floor of the Arctic Ocean. And all for one reason: the huge oil and gas wells in there. It's over 30 years since they signed that treaty not to touch them. But it is looking very shaky.

On the left is Ellesmere Island. It still has a fringe of winter ice. He scans it with his binoculars. Something catches his eye. A polar bear! Incredible! Unbelievable! He zooms in. It looks half dead, lying there on the ice. And so thin!

He'd better report it right away. That's his orders. With a sigh, he turns back to his office, to put in an urgent call.

▲ *Ellesmere Island in April 2000.*

▼ *A map of the Arctic in April 2000. Look how much was covered in ice.*

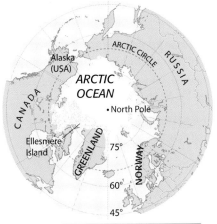

Key

▨	land
☐	ocean
☐	land and ocean covered in ice

Did you know?
- In 2000, there were about 27000 polar bears on the Earth.
- Over half were in Canada.

Did you know?
- Polar bears need ocean ice, to help them reach their main food: seals.

What if...
- ... the Earth just kept on getting hotter and hotter?

Your turn

1 Look at Molly's story.
  a In the story, what has changed in the UK by 2050, compared with today? List the changes. One is: *Farmers grow oranges*.
  b i Which of them do you think are 'good' changes? Underline these in one colour.
    ii Underline the 'bad' ones in another.
    iii If a change is good *and* bad, or if you can't tell, underline it in a third colour.
    iv Add a colour key.
  c Now discuss your answers with a partner. By the end, you may want to change some of your answers.
  d There is one big reason for most of the changes.
    i What is it? ii How could it make clothes cost more?

2 Look at the story of Aban and Numa.
  a Why have they left their village?
  b Do you think they will get to Europe? Give reasons.
  c If they do reach Europe, do you think they will find a country to take them in?

3 Captain Hanna's story is set in the Arctic Ocean.
  a Where is that ocean? Which countries surround it?
  b In what ways is it different in 2050 than in 2000?
  c Where is the North Pole? And it is real?

4 Captain Hanna sees a warship. What do you think it's doing there?

5 Captain Hanna has orders to report any polar bears he sees. Why do you think this is?

Our changing climate

This unit is about how our planet is warming up – and what the effects might be.

Getting warmer

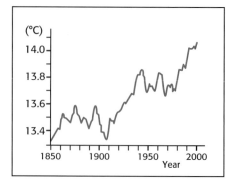

The air all around us, here in the lowest part of the atmosphere, is getting warmer.

We know that for sure, because scientists have been measuring its temperature for over 150 years.

This shows the measurements on a graph. Temperatures go up and down – but the overall trend is up.

It is happening all around the Earth. So we call it **global warming**.
It is happening faster in some places than others.

Is it a good thing?

It might seem good that the air is warming up. No more winter clothes!
But it's not so simple.

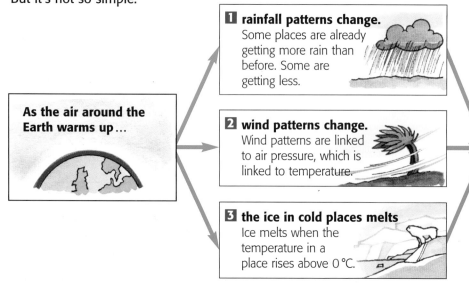

As the air around the Earth warms up...

1 rainfall patterns change.
Some places are already getting more rain than before. Some are getting less.

2 wind patterns change.
Wind patterns are linked to air pressure, which is linked to temperature.

3 the ice in cold places melts
Ice melts when the temperature in a place rises above 0 °C.

So world climates change.
This affects all living things:
- humans (including you)
- birds, fish, and other animals
- trees, crops, and other plants
- even bacteria and viruses.

So, what will the future bring?

The years 2001 to 2007 were seven of the world's eight hottest years, since records began in 1850.

Will it keep on getting warmer? How warm? And how will this affect us?

Scientists say it *will* keep getting warmer. They can't say how warm. Because that will partly depend on us.

But they try to predict what will happen, using computer models. The next page shows one set of predictions, and some likely effects. It is based on work by hundreds of scientists around the world.

Did you know?
- *The average global temperature in 2000 was 15.6 °C.*
- *A rise of 6 °C above that would kill off billions of humans.*

It could be like this!

Look at the map below. It shows one set of predictions for temperature rise, between 2000 and 2050. The deeper the red, the bigger the rise.

Look at the Arctic region, at the top of the map. It will still be cold there, in 2050. But temperatures could have risen by up to 4.5 °C, since 2000.

Now look at the boxes. They give the likely effects of all this warming.

- ◆ There will be more violent storms, and more floods.

- ◆ Ice in the Arctic and Antarctic will melt. The water from land ice will run into the sea, causing a rise in sea levels.

- ◆ Rising seas will drown low-lying coastal places. For example in Bangladesh, which is a low, flat country.

- ◆ There will be more heat waves in Europe and other places – and they'll kill hundreds of thousands of people.

How much temperatures may rise, between 2000 and 2050   **Temperature rise (°C)**

	6
	5.5
	5
	4.5
	4
	3.5
	3
	2.5
	2
	1.5
	1
	0.5
	0

- ◆ Some places will get much more rain, and some much less, than now.

- ◆ There will be millions more refugees, as people flee from floods, or drought and famine.

- ◆ Some places that depend on tourists will get too hot. Tourists will stay away.

- ◆ Some places will get too hot and dry to grow crops. This will cause famine.

- ◆ There may be wars over food and water.

- ◆ Other places will attract more and more tourists, as their climates 'improve'.

- ◆ Some places will grow new crops, that they were once too cold for.

- ◆ Animals and plants that can't cope (by moving, or adapting) will die out. (Will polar bears?)

- ◆ Diseases will spread, as insects and animals that carry them move to new places.

Your turn

1 Say what these terms mean – in your own words!
   a global warming   b climate change

2 The map above shows how much temperatures may rise between 2000 and 2050.
   a What age will you be by 2050?
   b How much warmer might it be then, compared with 2000: i in the UK? ii in Spain?
   iii on Ellesmere Island? iv in Russia?
   (Pages 140 – 141 and 71 will help.)

3 True or false? Give reasons.
   A Climate change will definitely not affect you.
   B Climate change will have social effects.
   C Climate change won't have any economic effects.
   D Climate change won't affect the environment.
   E No one will benefit from climate change.
   F Rising sea levels won't affect the UK.

4 Look at those effects of global warming, in the boxes. Which do *you* think would be the worst one? Why?

What's causing global warming?

Is global warming only natural? Or is it our fault? Find out more here.

The big argument

We depend on scientists to tell us what's causing global warming.
But it is a very hard question. And they don't all agree on the answer:

What's the final verdict?

Arguments still go on. But a large team of scientists from around the world
was asked to look at all the data. In November 2007, it reported:

> *Most* of the increase in global
> temperatures since the mid-20th
> century is *very likely* due to the
> increase in greenhouse gases.

We're over 90% sure they are the main cause.

Did you know?
♦ Without greenhouse gases, the average world temperature would be about -18°C.

So what are greenhouse gases?

Greenhouse gases are any gases that
trap heat around the Earth. Like this:

1 The sun sends out energy, as light and UV rays.

2 These warm the Earth. The Earth reflects some of the energy again, as heat.

3 Some of this heat escapes to the outer atmosphere.

4 But some is absorbed by the molecules of greenhouse gases.

5 They re-emit it in all directions, including back to the Earth.

6 So the air, and Earth, get warmer.

SUN

ATMOSPHERE

greenhouse gases

EARTH

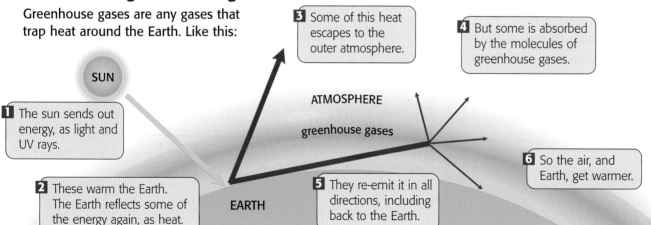

We *need* greenhouse gases. Without them, all the heat from the Earth
would escape. So we could not survive at night, when there's no sunlight.
But now their level is rising fast. So the Earth is getting warmer.

Which gases are they?

These are many greenhouse gases. These are the four main ones.

Carbon dioxide, CO_2 It's the one that worries people most. Because it's the one we are adding to the air fastest.

You breathe out carbon dioxide. Plants and trees take it in. (They also give out some.) It used to be in balance, in the air. But we add extra, every time we burn …

… coal, oil, and gas (the fossil fuels) and petrol and diesel. Plus we are cutting down forests, so there are fewer trees to take carbon dioxide in.

So the level of carbon dioxide in the air has been rising. Ever since the Industrial Revolution, over 200 years ago. Now it's rising faster than ever. It is no longer in balance.

Methane, CH_4 This is the 'natural gas' piped to homes. Some escapes from oil and gas wells. It also forms in landfill sites, when stuff rots. It's given off from rice paddy fields. And when cows belch. And when animal waste breaks down.

Methane is far more powerful than carbon dioxide, as a greenhouse gas. But there is much less of it in the air.

Nitrous oxide, N_2O It is produced by bacteria in the soil. When we add fertilisers, they produce more! It is a very powerful greenhouse gas – but the level in the air is low.

Water vapour, H_2O It forms when water evaporates from the oceans. As the air warms up, more will evaporate. So it will play a growing part in global warming. And we can't control it!

Did you know?
♦ Australia's cattle and sheep give out about 3 million tonnes of methane a year.

Did you know?
♦ The world gives out over 25 billion tonnes of carbon dioxide a year, from burning fossil fuels.

Your turn

1 In the past, the sun may have caused global warming (or cooling). How do you think it could it do that?

2 The Earth's path around the sun changes over time:

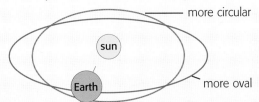

That could cause a change in climates. See if you can explain why.

3 Look back at that verdict from the team of scientists, on page 74. Do you think it is wise to believe them? Give your reasons.

4 Explain what greenhouse gases are:
   a in 20 – 25 words
   b in 10 – 14 words
   c in just 6 words

5 All these statements are about greenhouse gases. Copy and complete them:
   a We would die without greenhouse gases, because …
   b Greenhouse gases can harm us, because …
   c The level of greenhouse gases in the air is …
   d The more farming we humans do, the more …
   e When we drive our cars, we …

6 Which greenhouse gas(es):
   a do you think *you* add to the air?
   b do you think we could cut back on?

More about carbon dioxide

In this unit you'll learn about the things we do, that produce carbon dioxide.

CO$_2$, the main culprit

Carbon dioxide is the greenhouse gas that is causing most concern – because we pump so much of it into the air.

Carbon dioxide forms when we burn anything containing carbon. Such as:

- coal, oil, and gas (the fossil fuels)
- petrol, diesel, kerosene (obtained from oil)
- things like wood and straw
- ethanol, an alcohol made from crops such as wheat and sugar cane.

We burn all of those things as fuels. Look at these examples.

Did you know?
- Two billion people around the world depend on fuel wood and animal dung, for their cooking.

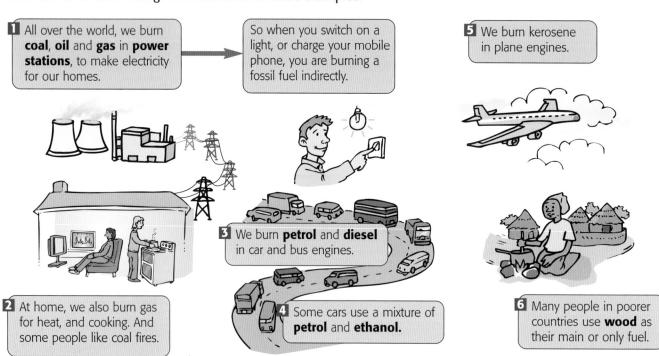

1 All over the world, we burn **coal**, **oil** and **gas** in **power stations**, to make electricity for our homes.

So when you switch on a light, or charge your mobile phone, you are burning a fossil fuel indirectly.

5 We burn kerosene in plane engines.

3 We burn **petrol** and **diesel** in car and bus engines.

2 At home, we also burn gas for heat, and cooking. And some people like coal fires.

4 Some cars use a mixture of **petrol** and **ethanol.**

6 Many people in poorer countries use **wood** as their main or only fuel.

So carbon dioxide is produced in each case.

Different countries, different amounts

All countries pump carbon dioxide into the air, by burning fuels that contain carbon.

But the amount varies a great deal from country to country.

Look at this bar graph. It shows the average amount of carbon dioxide produced per person, in different countries, in 2004. Look at the differences.

Can you guess why a person in Kenya produces so little, compared with a person in the UK?

The figures change from year to year. They are rising fast for China and India, because these countries are developing fast. Lots of new factories are being set up. More and more people are buying cars, washing machines, computers …

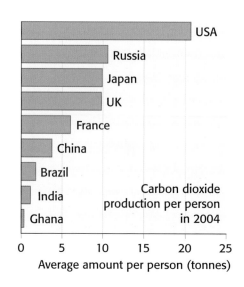

USA
Russia
Japan
UK
France
China
Brazil
India
Ghana

Carbon dioxide production per person in 2004

0   5   10   15   20   25
Average amount per person (tonnes)

The trouble is …

The trouble is this …

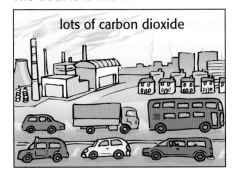

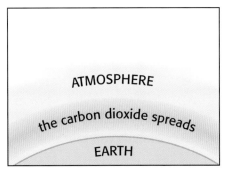

When we burn fuels containing carbon, the carbon dioxide gas goes into the air. But it does not hang around in one place for long.

It is carried away by winds, and spreads through the lower atmosphere. So its warming effect is felt everywhere.

The result is that people in poorer countries, who burn far less fuel than we do, still suffer from the effects of global warming.

Local actions, global effects

So, when you leave the light on in your room, or the TV on standby, you may be affecting someone far away, on the other side of the world. It's an example of **local actions, global effects**.

People in poorer countries may not be able to cope with the disasters global warming will bring: like floods, and drought, and crop loss. Coping with these could cost billions.

Did you know?

♦ *Oil, coal, and gas together provide about 80% of the world's energy.*

Your turn

1 How much do you depend on burning fuels? Let's explore.

   a

   Things I do on a typical school day
   get up
   turn light on
   take shower
   dry hair
   eat cornflakes
   catch bus to school

   Make a list like this for your typical school day. Fill in the main things you do.
   (Do you phone a lot? Or go on the computer?)

   b Now underline any activities that depend on burning fuels. Think carefully!
   (For example, turning the light on links you to a power station, where a fuel is burned.)

   c Look at the things you underlined. Where is the fuel burned? Mark the ones where it's burned:
   i where you are (for example, gas in your home)
   ii somewhere else (for example, in a power station)
   Mark them in any way you wish. You could use * and **, for example. Then add a key to explain.

2 Look at your list. Do you depend a lot on burning fuels? Draw a scale like this, and mark an **X** on it, for you.

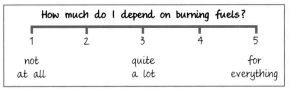

3 Look at the bar graph on page 76.
   a Which of the nine countries produced most carbon dioxide per person, in 2004? See if you can explain why.
   b Which produced least? Try to explain this too.
   c About how many times more did a person in the UK produce, than a person in China?
   d In 2004, China had 1300 million people. The UK had 60 million. Using the bar graph, see if you can work out a rough figure for the *total output* of carbon dioxide that year for:
   i China   ii the UK

4 Copy and complete these sentences:
   a 'Local actions, global effects' means …
   b The burning of fossil fuels is an example of 'local actions, global effects' because …

So can we stop global warming?

In this unit you'll find out whether we can stop global warming.
And if we can't – what *can* we do?

Can we stop global warming?

No.

We can't stop global warming. Not even if we stop burning fuels right now. The extra carbon dioxide in the air already will cause temperatures to rise by at least 1 °C.

But we *can* try to reduce the amount of carbon dioxide we produce, to limit temperature rises. It's the best we can hope for.

So, what *are* we doing? We are burning more fuels than ever. So we are producing more carbon dioxide than ever. So global warming is speeding up.

And here is the big worry. As the world heats up we will reach tipping points, when things suddenly get far worse.

For example, if it gets hot enough, trees will die. So they will stop taking in carbon dioxide. On decay, they will give out carbon dioxide. Its level will shoot up even faster.

And then, one day, it may be too late. Temperatures could rise out of control. Climates would change drastically. Living things could not cope. We would not recover.

We must take urgent action now. What are we waiting for?

From science reports, 2008

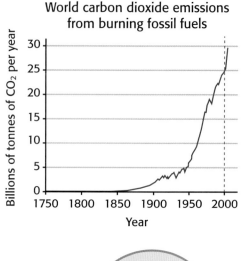

World carbon dioxide emissions from burning fossil fuels

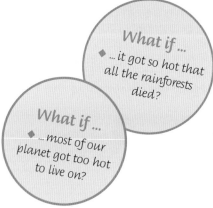

What if...
◆ ...it got so hot that all the rainforests died?

What if...
◆ ...most of our planet got too hot to live on?

So what are our options?

Here are some options. What do you think?

A Do nothing. Just carry on as we are.

B Find ways to take carbon dioxide out of the air.

C Cut back on the amount of carbon dioxide we each produce.

D Stop some sunlight from reaching the Earth.

E Stop the world's population growing.

▲ *Outside a United Nations meeting about climate change, in Indonesia in 2007.*

▲ *Inside, government ministers from over 180 countries try to agree on plans for tackling climate change.*

Your turn

1 Look at the graph on page 78. It shows world carbon dioxide emissions from burning fossil fuels.
  a What does *emissions* mean?
  b Is this true or false? Give evidence from the graph to back up your answer.
   i Emissions are rising.
   ii Emissions are rising faster than ever, since 2000.
   iii About 5 times more carbon dioxide was emitted in 2000 than in 1950, from burning fossil fuels.

2 Look at each fact below, in turn. Could it help to explain why carbon dioxide emissions are rising? Give reasons.
  a The world's population is rising fast.
  b Many countries that were once very poor are now developing quite fast.
  c Flights are getting cheaper and cheaper.

3 Think about the options at the bottom of page 78.
  a Which one do you think is the best?
  b Which one do you think is the worst?
  c Write them out fully, in your chosen order, from best to worst.

Options	
best	....
↑	....
	....
	....
worst	....

4 Now give reasons for the order you chose. Like this:

I put option ...... first because ....
I put option ...... second, because ....

5 Look at the first photo above. Which option from page 78 have those people chosen?

6 These actions could help to slow down global warming.

   1 Give out free bikes to everyone.
   2 Build more windfarms, for electricity.
   3 Breed plants that will gobble up carbon dioxide.
   4 Don't turn on the heating. Just put on warm clothes.
   5 Put big taxes on air travel.
   6 Allow homes to have electricity for only 6 hours a day.
   7 Shut down all power stations that use coal, oil, or gas.
   8 Turn off all the town and city lights at night.
   9 Find a way to bury carbon dioxide under the ocean.
   10 Pass a law that women can have only one child each.
   11 Ban international events like the Olympic Games.
   12 Shoot millions of small mirrors into space, to reflect some sunlight away.

  a Match each action to an option from page 78, using a table like the one on the right.
  b Which actions above depend on:
   i scientists?
   ii the government?
  c Which two do you think would cause most protest from people? Why?
  d Which two would you choose first, if you were in charge? Why?

Option	Action
A	....
B	....
C	1, ...
D	....
E	....

7 Now write a list of things *you* can do on your own, to help limit global warming. Your answers for question 1 on page 77 may help.

GLOBAL WARMING WARRIOR

Where should we get our energy?

The big picture

This chapter looks at one thing we all depend on: energy.
These are the big ideas behind the chapter:

◆ We use energy to cook, light our homes, drive cars, and so on.

◆ We use a lot of energy in one very convenient form: electricity.

◆ We get our electricity from a mix of sources – but mostly by burning fossil fuels.

◆ We are trying to cut back on our use of fossil fuels. (Global warming is one big reason.)

◆ So we need to develop other sources of energy, in their place.

Your goals for this chapter

By the end of this chapter you should be able to answer these questions:

◆ What do these terms mean, and what examples of each can I give?

fossil fuel   nuclear fuel   biofuel
a renewable source of energy   a non-renewable source of energy

◆ Why do we like electricity so much, as a form of energy?

◆ How is electricity made?

◆ Why are fossil fuels so important in our lives – and why is oil the most important?

◆ Why is it a good idea to cut back on using fossil fuels? (At least four reasons.)

◆ Which energy sources are available to us, in the UK? And which of them are renewable?

◆ What are the main good and bad points about nuclear power?

◆ What are the main good and bad points about biofuels?

◆ How does solar power work? And what are its special advantages, for poorer countries?

And then …

When you finish this chapter, come back to this page, and see if you have met your goals!

Did you know?
◆ Many young people like you, in poorer countries, spend hours every day searching for firewood.

Did you know?
◆ We import natural gas from Norway, through an undersea pipe – 1200 km long!

Did you know?
◆ The Sun sends more energy to the Earth in one hour than we humans use in a year!

What if...
◆ ... we could get all the energy we need, for everything, just from sunlight?

Your chapter starter

Look at the photo on page 80.

What is that structure? And what can you see below it?

Why did they put that structure there?

About how tall would you say it is?

Has it got anything to do with you?

Don't run out on me.

Energy, fuels, and electricity

Here you will review energy and its sources. You will learn more about electricity. And then you will identify renewable energy sources.

We need energy!

You know from science class that energy can take many forms – heat, light, sound, electricity, movement, and chemical energy. And it can change from one form to another.

We need energy. For cooking, heating and lighting our homes, listening to music, moving cars, phoning friends. We mostly use **fuels** to provide it.

Fuels

Fuels are just a store of energy. All these are used as fuels:

◆ the fossil fuels – gas, coal and oil (and things like petrol, made from oil)
◆ nuclear fuels
◆ wood, straw, and even rubbish.

We usually burn fuels, to release their energy. But not nuclear fuels. They contain unstable atoms, and we split these to release energy. (See Unit 6.4 for more on nuclear energy.)

Electricity: energy made easy

There's one form of energy we all use, every day: electricity. How is it made? Easy! Just move a magnet inside a coil of wire.

In a power station they use a large magnet called an **electromagnet**. They use steam to make the magnet spin, and a **fuel** to make the steam.

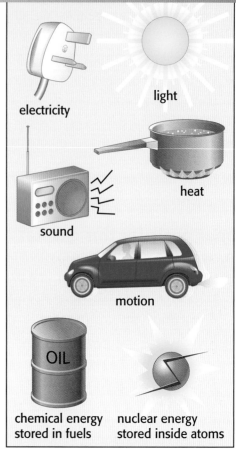

▲ *All are forms of energy.*

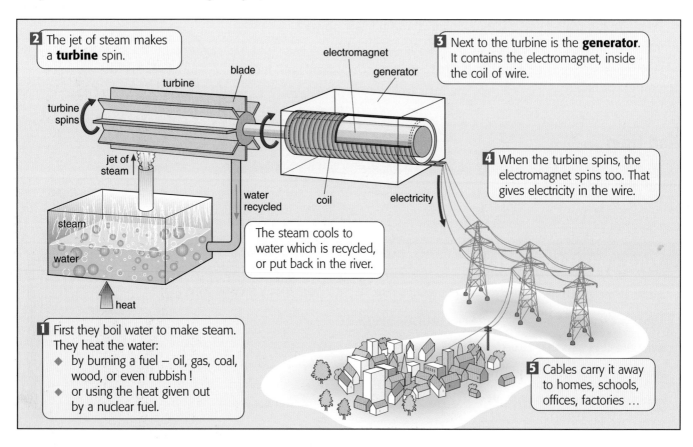

2 The jet of steam makes a **turbine** spin.

3 Next to the turbine is the **generator**. It contains the electromagnet, inside the coil of wire.

4 When the turbine spins, the electromagnet spins too. That gives electricity in the wire.

The steam cools to water which is recycled, or put back in the river.

1 First they boil water to make steam. They heat the water:
◆ by burning a fuel – oil, gas, coal, wood, or even rubbish!
◆ or using the heat given out by a nuclear fuel.

5 Cables carry it away to homes, schools, offices, factories …

It doesn't have to be steam

You make electricity by spinning a turbine – in any way you like!
You don't have to use steam. You can use a river, or the wind, or the sea.

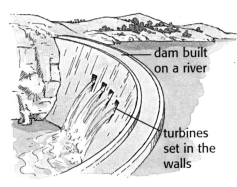

In a **hydroelectric** station, fast-flowing **water** spins the turbines.

On a **wind farm**, the wind spins them, by turning the blades.

1 The waves move up and down.

2 This makes the trapped air move, and it spins the turbine.

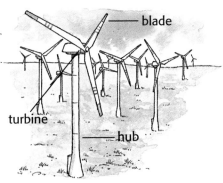

In the sea, **waves** and the **tide** can make a turbine spin.

The electricity can then be fed into the **National Grid**. That's the network of cables that carries electricity around the UK.

Renewable or not?

Coal, oil and gas are called **fossil fuels**, because they are the remains of plants and sea animals that lived millions of years ago. We are using them up very fast. One day, there won't be any more we can access. So we call them a **non-renewable resource**.

It's the same with nuclear fuels. The Earth contains only a certain amount. When we dig them all up, that's it!

But wood is different. It won't run out – we can keep growing new trees. So wood is a **renewable** resource. What about the wind? Is it?

When will we run out?
This is what some experts think:

At our present rate of use we could run out of …	in about …
oil	40 years
gas	60 years
coal	250 years

Your turn

1 Energy can change from one form to another.
What change takes place when you:
a turn on a light? b use a gas cooker?

2 What is: a a fuel? b a fossil fuel? c nuclear fuel?

3 See if you can draw a flow chart to show how electricity is generated in a power station, using gas as a fuel.

4 We spend billions turning other fuels into electricity.
a Why do we like electricity so much?
b What advantages does it have over: i oil? ii gas?

5 Copy the table on the right. Then complete it by putting ticks (for *yes*) and crosses (for *no*) in the right places.

6 Look at the pie chart for 2006.
About how much of our electricity came from:
a nuclear fuel? b oil? c coal?
d fossil fuels? e hydro and other renewables?
Try the easiest ones first. All the answers are in this list:
*about three quarters about 40 % a fifth (20%)
one twentieth (5%) one fiftieth (2%)*

Sources of energy

	A fossil fuel?	Used to make electricity?	A renewable resource?
gas	✓		
oil			
coal			
wood			
nuclear fuel			
river			
the wind			
waves			
the tide			

Sources of UK electricity, 2006

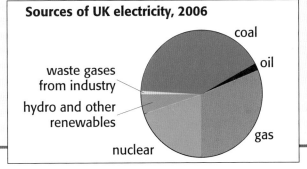

A red card for the fossil fuels?

Here you will review the problems linked to fossil fuels.

You depend on the fossil fuels

You depend on the fossil fuels – coal, gas, and oil – for your lifestyle. And most of all, on oil.

4 You depend on petrol, diesel, and kerosene (all from oil), to get around.

1 The electricity you use depends mainly on fossil fuels.
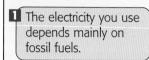

5 And you use gas, or electricity, for cooking and heating.

2 The factories that make the things you love are run on fossil fuels.
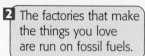

3 And dozens of the things you use start off as oil …

… for example shampoo, shower gel, and things that are all, or partly, plastic: comb, toothbrush, watch, trainers, raincoat, mobile, TV …

The trouble is …

The fossil fuels make our lives comfortable. But they cause problems too. Look at the yellow cards, A – D.

A Global warming

The fossil fuels give off carbon dioxide gas when they burn. And this is making the Earth warm up.

We call it **global warming**.

It is causing climate change around the world. It will lead to severe storms and floods, famine, and other disasters.

See Chapter 5 for more.

▲ *Power stations produce a huge amount of carbon dioxide. (But the white clouds are steam.)*

B Other damage to the environment

1 Acid rain

Other gases also form when the fossil fuels burn. Some are acidic, and can damage your lungs. These also dissolve in rain to give **acid rain**.

Acid rain kills trees and plants on land, and fish and other living things in lakes and rivers.

2 Other pollutants

The burning fuels give off smoke, soot and other particles that get everywhere, including into your lungs.

3 And more …

We can harm the environment when we dig up, and move, the fossil fuels. For example, oil spills do a lot of damage.

▲ *A victim of an oil spill from a tanker at sea. It will die if no one helps.*

C Problems with supply

1 We can't be sure of getting them

Just think about this:

- Over 100 countries have no oil of their own.
- And most countries with oil do not have enough, so have to buy some (like the UK does).
- Only about 15 countries have lots of oil to sell.

So what if countries refuse to sell us oil (or gas, or coal)? Or if there's a war? Wars can stop supplies.

▲ *An oil refinery on fire, during the Iraq war.*
(Iraq has the fourth largest oil reserves in the world.)

2 And anyway, they are running out!

The fossil fuels will run out one day. Experts say oil will run out first. Perhaps in even less than 40 years. What will we do then?

D And money problems!

The world is using more and more fossil fuel every year, as its population grows, and countries develop.

So countries are competing with each other to buy the fossil fuels. And this is pushing up prices.

When the prices of fossil fuels rise, so do other prices. We have to pay more for things like:

- food
- clothing
- electricity and petrol
- train and bus fares

It affects everyone. The poorest are hit hardest.

▲ *It all costs more as the prices of fossil fuels rise.*

Is it time to send the fossil fuels off?

So, the fossil fuels give us problems. Most countries want to cut back on them. But we can't *stop* using them until we have other energy sources to replace them. That will take years.

All over the world, people are working hard to develop other energy sources. Which ones can we use, here in the UK? Find out in the following units.

Did you know?

- *If everyone in the world used oil at the same rate as people in the USA, it could run out in eight years.*

Your turn

1 Fossil fuels play a big part in your life. Explain why.
2 Of all the ways the fossil fuels help us, which one is the most important for *you*? Why?
3 Look at the pie chart on the right. Which fossil fuel does the world depend on most? See if you can explain why.
4 The four yellow cards give the problems linked to fossil fuels.
   a Find two examples of environmental problems.
   b Give one example of an economic problem.
   c Which do you rate as the *main* problem? Why?
   d Which of the problems are likely to affect you?
5 A rise in the price of oil can lead to a rise in the price of clothing. See if you can explain why. (Try a flow chart?)
6 Shock! The government has banned the use of all fossil fuels in the UK, from today!
   How do you think your life will have changed:
   a in one week from now? b in one year from now?

Where the world got its energy in 2005

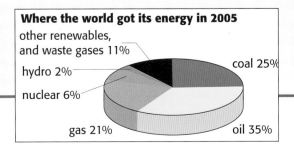

other renewables, and waste gases 11%

hydro 2%

nuclear 6%

gas 21%

coal 25%

oil 35%

Here you'll learn more about our sources of energy, here in the UK.

Lucky us!

We are lucky, here in the UK. We have a choice of energy sources.
Look at this drawing, and the next page. Then try 'Your turn'.

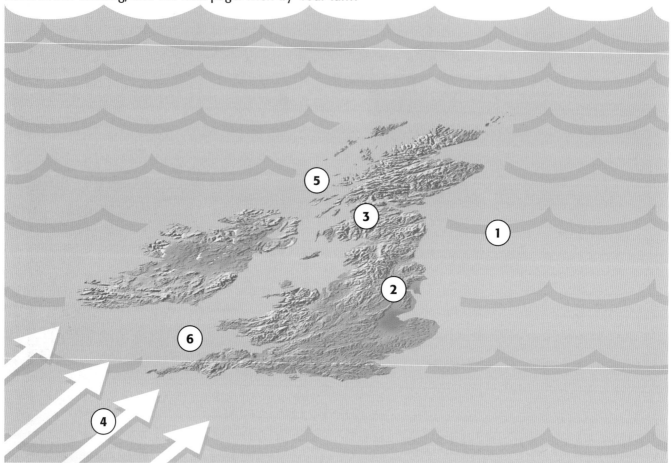

⑦

Your turn

1 Look at those energy sources, in the boxes on page 87.
  a Which ones will *not* run out on us?
  b Which ones are available:
     i off the coast?   ii on land?
  c Which ones can we use for electricity?

2 a Most of our hydroelectricity comes from Scotland.
     Can you explain why? (Page 139 may help.)
  b We can't increase our hydroelectricity much. Why not?

3 When we use an energy source, it usually has *some*
  impact on the environment. For example it may pollute
  the air, or scare birds, or spoil a view.
  Look at the sources of energy on page 87.
  See if you can arrange them in order of their impact on
  the environment. (Use all you know already.)
  Start with the one you think has the least impact.

4 We use a mix of
  energy sources,
  for our electricity.
  This pie chart
  shows the mix
  for 2006, again.

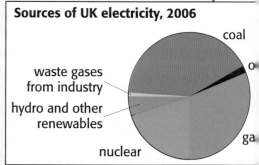

Sources of UK electricity, 2006

coal

o

waste gases
from industry

hydro and other
renewables

ga

nuclear

  a What do you think of the mix in the pie chart?
  b i Now sketch a very rough pie chart for the mix *you*
      would like us to have, in future. Label the slices.
    ii Explain why you chose this mix.

5 How could we use wave power to power a car?
  Think of a way to do this. Draw a labelled sketch to
  show your idea.

Our energy sources

① Oil and gas

- We have oil and gas in the North Sea.
- But they're starting to run out.
- Now the UK has to import some, to meet its needs.

② Coal

- Our coal industry was once huge – but it declined.
- Now we import most of the coal we need.
- But we still have quite a lot of coal left, and some new mines are being opened.

③ Hydro (rivers)

- All our big fast-flowing rivers have dams for hydroelectricity, already.

④ Wind-power

- The UK is a windy country.
- For now, the wind is our main new hope, for electricity.
- In 2008 we had around 170 wind farms – and nearly 400 more on the way.
- Some of them are out at sea.

⑤ Wave power

- The waves all around us could provide plenty of electricity.
- But wave power is still at a very early stage.

- Here is one device on trial. The waves move it up and down. As it moves, a turbine spins – and we get electricity.

⑥ Tidal power

- We could also use the tides to give electricity.
- But tidal power is also at a very early stage.

- This shows one idea. As the tides rise and fall, the blades turn, and spin a turbine.

⑦ Solar power

- More and more of us are making electricity from sunlight, using PV cells.
- Just put them on your roof!

So where *should* we get our energy?

As you saw, there are problems with the fossil fuels. But we can't stop using them, until we can get enough energy, cheaply enough, from other sources.

The government has set a target: 15% of our electricity from renewable sources by 2020, to help fight global warming.

We will always need a mix of energy sources. But the mix will change as we develop sources ④– ⑦, above. Scientists are working hard on this.

We will still get some electricity from **nuclear fuel** too (Unit 6.4). And we will use some **biofuels** for transport (Unit 6.6).

More nuclear power?

Here you'll learn about nuclear power, and the pros and cons.

Nuclear fuel

Here in the UK, we get about one fifth of our electricity from nuclear fuel. So how does it work?

A nuclear fuel is just a metal compound. But it has a special feature – the metal atoms are unstable. Sooner or later they break down. Like this:

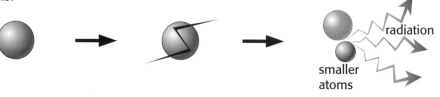

radiation

smaller atoms

+

1 This is an unstable atom.

2 It breaks down into two smaller atoms, in a nuclear reaction.

3 As it breaks down it gives out **radiation** (a mixture of tiny particles, and rays) …

4 … plus a huge amount of energy – and that's why we use it!

We call the unstable atoms **radioactive**, because they give out radiation.

The main nuclear fuel is **uranium dioxide**. There are very tiny amounts of this compound in most rocks, even in the UK. But some countries, such as Australia and Canada, have large deposits. So we buy it from them.

In a nuclear power station

Those unstable atoms break down naturally, over time. But in a nuclear power station, we *force* them to break down, by shooting tiny particles called neutrons at them. (You met neutrons in science class.)

This gives us an enormous amount of energy, mostly in the form of heat.

The energy is used to heat water, to give steam. The steam spins a turbine. And the result is … electricity! (Look back at the diagram on page 82.)

▲ *At work in a nuclear power station.*

The good things about nuclear power

◆ A tiny amount of nuclear fuel gives an enormous amount of energy.

◆ No carbon dioxide is given out. So it does not add to global warming,

◆ It does not produce much waste.

Compare these two power stations. Both give the same amount of electricity:

Power station	Amount of fuel used in a year	Amount of waste produced in a year
nuclear	about 25 tonnes of uranium dioxide	about one tonne of radioactive waste
coal-fired	about 3 million tonnes of coal	about 7 million tonnes of waste – carbon dioxide, sulphur dioxide and other harmful gases, soot, and ash

▲ *The Sizewell nuclear power station, in Suffolk. The white dome is above the* **reactor** *(where the atoms break down).*

The bad things about nuclear power

◆ Radiation is very dangerous. A big blast of it will kill you. Even a small dose can cause cancer.

◆ The waste material from the nuclear reaction is also radioactive. So it is very dangerous. It can remain dangerous for hundreds of years.

The UK's dilemma

The UK has nine working nuclear power stations. By 2023, only one of these will still be running. That could leave us short of electricity!

So the government wants new power stations. And for building to start soon. (It takes at least 10 years to build one.) But what do people think?

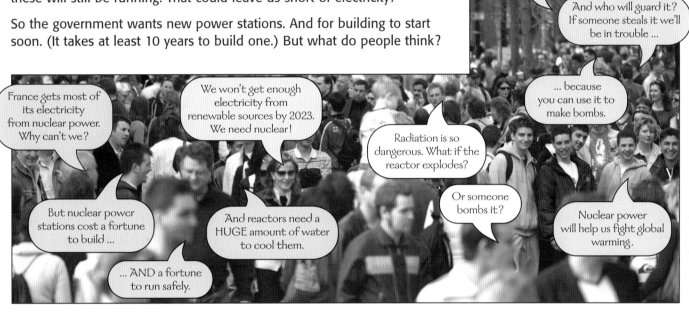

They plan to bury the dangerous waste – but where?

Not near me, I hope!

And who will guard it? If someone steals it we'll be in trouble ...

... because you can use it to make bombs.

France gets most of its electricity from nuclear power. Why can't we?

We won't get enough electricity from renewable sources by 2023. We need nuclear!

Radiation is so dangerous. What if the reactor explodes?

But nuclear power stations cost a fortune to build ...

And reactors need a HUGE amount of water to cool them.

Or someone bombs it?

Nuclear power will help us fight global warming.

... AND a fortune to run safely.

The Chernobyl disaster

Nuclear power stations cause no problems, most of the time. But in 1986, a reactor exploded in the nuclear power station at Chernobyl, in Ukraine. And a plume of deadly particles shot out through the damaged roof.

56 people died soon after the explosion. Up to 10 000 people who were in the area died later, or are still dying, from cancers caused by the radiation.

The deadly particles were carried far away by the wind. Some even ended up on high land in the UK, on sheep farms. The sheep were tested for radioactivity. Some were above the safe limit. So the farmers were not allowed to sell these for meat.

After the disaster, people were moved out of the Chernobyl area. And told to stay away, for ever. Even so, some have moved back to their homes again.

▲ *Not in favour?*

Your turn

1 What is a nuclear fuel?

2 Copy and complete these:
   a I think the best thing about nuclear power is …
   b I think the worst thing about nuclear power is …
   c The government wants new nuclear power stations because …

3 You have to decide *where* to put new nuclear power stations, in the UK. What kind of place will you look for? The speech bubbles above may help.

4 Look at this person's opinion. Do you agree? Explain.

Global warming is more dangerous than nuclear power!

A wind farm for Corfe Castle?

Here you'll find out more about wind farms, and explore a proposal for one.

Wind power: little and large

You could put up just a single wind turbine on your roof, for electricity for your home. Thousands of homes have them already.

Or build a **wind farm** of turbines. Our largest onshore one (so far), is near Glasgow. It has 140 turbines, to power 200 000 homes.

You could build it offshore, like this. One with 341 turbines is planned for the Thames Estuary, near London. It will power a million homes.

Wind turbines don't burn fuels. So no carbon dioxide. Great! Even so, people often object to wind farms. Usually because they think they will disturb wildlife, or be too noisy, or spoil a lovely view.

So should Corfe Castle have a wind farm?

The OS map opposite shows the village of Corfe Castle in Dorset.

The village is less than 5 km from the south coast, as the crow flies. The castle itself was built by the Normans. It once belonged to Henry VIII. But his daughter, Elizabeth I, sold it. And now it's in ruins.

Turbowind is a wind energy company. (An imaginary one!) It wants to build a small wind farm at Corfe Castle. Just six turbines. The pink dots on the map show where it wants to place them. A good idea? Over to you!

> **Factbox**
> ◆ The prevailing wind at Corfe Castle is from the south (the coast).
> ◆ High open land is best for turbines. (But you *can* get enough wind on low open land too.)
> ◆ The Turbowind turbines are 120 m tall, from base to wing tip (or 15 times as high as a two-storey house).
> ◆ You hear a 'beat' as the blades turn. So it's best if a turbine is at least 400 m from the nearest home.

Your turn

1 First, find the ruins of the castle, on the map. (There is a blue pointer to them.) Why did the Normans choose that site for a castle? Think up some reasons.

2 Do you think the village attracts many tourists? Give your evidence. Page 138 may help.

3 Now look at Challow Hill. Why did Turbowind choose that site for a wind farm? Give as many reasons as you can. The OS map, and the factbox above, give clues.

4 Pretend you are each of these, in turn. Write down how you feel about the wind farm, and why:
   a the owner of Challow Farm, south of the site
   b the owner of the hotel near Corfe Castle station
   c a teenager staying in the campsite in 9482
   d the manager of the Brenscombe Outdoor Centre
   e a tourist taking a ride on the steam train
   f a sheep grazing on Challow Hill.

5 You work for Turbowind. You will be in charge of bringing the turbines in, by road. Your instructions are:

> ● Use long trucks, like the one in photo **B**.
> ● Use the A351 or the B3351 road, in either direction.
> ● Build an access road onto Challow Hill itself.

   a Draw a sketch map showing the four possible routes the trucks could take.
   b Mark in any problems you can see, on each route.
   c Then pick out the route you think is best, and show where you will put your access road.

6 Purbeck Council will meet to decide about the wind farm. Should it give permission, or turn the plan down? Write a short speech to make to the council, giving *your* opinion, and your two main reasons.

▲ A turbine blade on the way to a wind farm site.

◀ Corfe Castle village. Spot the castle! Can you give a grid reference for the place where the photographer stood?

What are biofuels? And are they a good idea? Find out here.

What are biofuels?

Biofuels are liquids made from plant material, to use as fuels for cars, trucks and planes. Ethanol is an example. This is how it's made:

First grow your plants. This farmer is growing **corn**, on his farm in the USA. (Here we call it **maize**.) He's growing it for ethanol, not food.

At the biofuel plant, the corn kernels are ground up. Water and enzymes are added. The enzymes turn the corn starch into ethanol.

The ethanol is distilled off. It is mixed with petrol. And you fill up at the petrol station. (But first, check it's okay for your engine.)

It's not just corn. You can make ethanol from other things too. In Brazil they make it from sugar cane.

Why bother?

Ethanol contains carbon. So when it burns it gives out … ?

Yes, carbon dioxide.

But they call it a **carbon neutral** fuel. This drawing shows why.

Overall, the ethanol does not add more carbon dioxide to the air. Petrol is different. When you burn petrol in a car engine, you release carbon dioxide that was locked away millions of years ago.

1 Carbon dioxide is given out when ethanol burns, but …

2 … taken in by more corn as it grows, in the process called **photosynthesis**.

Will you use biofuels?

Sooner or later, you'll travel with the help of a biofuel. Petrol with added ethanol is already on sale at some petrol pumps in the UK.

▲ *Going nutty? In February 2008, this plane flew from London to Amsterdam, with the help of a biofuel made from coconuts and nuts.*

▲ *His engine has been adapted to run on used oil from the chip shop!*

Are they *really* a good idea?

Biofuels sound great. But how great are they?
Let's go to the USA, where ethanol is big business.
Follow the numbers.

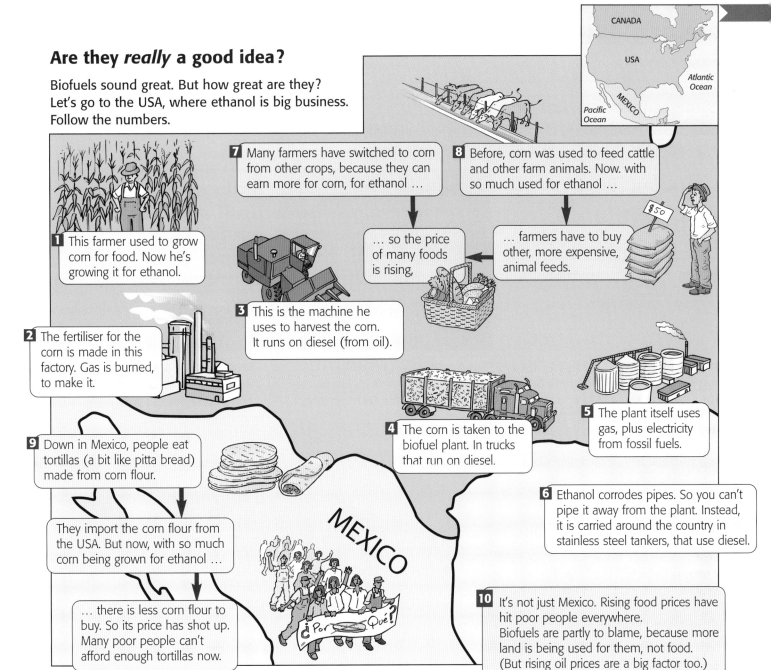

1 This farmer used to grow corn for food. Now he's growing it for ethanol.

2 The fertiliser for the corn is made in this factory. Gas is burned, to make it.

3 This is the machine he uses to harvest the corn. It runs on diesel (from oil).

4 The corn is taken to the biofuel plant. In trucks that run on diesel.

5 The plant itself uses gas, plus electricity from fossil fuels.

6 Ethanol corrodes pipes. So you can't pipe it away from the plant. Instead, it is carried around the country in stainless steel tankers, that use diesel.

7 Many farmers have switched to corn from other crops, because they can earn more for corn, for ethanol …

… so the price of many foods is rising,

8 Before, corn was used to feed cattle and other farm animals. Now. with so much used for ethanol …

… farmers have to buy other, more expensive, animal feeds.

9 Down in Mexico, people eat tortillas (a bit like pitta bread) made from corn flour.

They import the corn flour from the USA. But now, with so much corn being grown for ethanol …

… there is less corn flour to buy. So its price has shot up. Many poor people can't afford enough tortillas now.

10 It's not just Mexico. Rising food prices have hit poor people everywhere.
Biofuels are partly to blame, because more land is being used for them, not food.
(But rising oil prices are a big factor too.)

Your turn

1 What is a *biofuel*? Name one.

2 Copy and complete this sentence:

   Ethanol made from corn is called a carbon-neutral fuel because …

3 The USA imports about 10 million barrels of oil a day. See if you can give two reasons why its government is so keen on ethanol from corn.

4 a Now look at drawings 2-6 above. In which stages are fossil fuels burned? Give their numbers.

   b Do you think ethanol is *really* a carbon-neutral fuel? Give your reasons.

5 Lots of American farmers now grow corn for ethanol.
   a This has affected people in Mexico. Explain how.
   b It has also led to a rise in meat prices, in the USA. See if you can explain why.

6 Look at this person's placard. What does the slogan mean? Give its meaning in your own words, as a full sentence.

FEED PEOPLE, NOT CARS!

7 Scientists are working on a new biofuel for cars. It's made by bacteria that feed on waste plant material. Like potato skins, waste paper, and your old cotton socks! Do you think this fuel is a good idea? Decide, and give your reasons. (You could give them as a spider map.)

Here you'll learn more about solar power, and how it is being used.

Straight from the sun

Solar power means energy from sunlight. When the sunlight strikes a **photovoltaic cell** or **PV cell**, a current is produced.

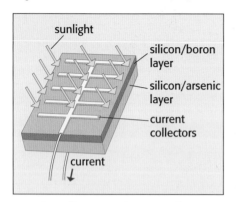

Here's a diagram of a PV cell. You put the cell in sunlight. Wires carry the current away – and you use it to light or heat a room.

You can buy PV cells just for electricity for your own house. For example in the form of roof tiles, like these.

Or set up a big solar power plant in a sunny place, like here in the USA. Cables carry the electricity to many homes.

As you can see, no fuel is burned – so no carbon dioxide! And you can store up the electricity from a PV cell in a big battery, to use later.

Solar power in the UK

The UK is not the sunniest place. But even on a cloudy day, we get enough sunlight for solar power.

PV cells were invented for satellites. At first they cost a lot. But they are getting cheaper. So more are being used – to power homes and parking meters, to light up bus shelters, and so on. You can even buy jackets with solar panels, for charging your mobile.

So … the use of solar power is growing.

▲ A solar panel for charging a mobile.

Good news for developing countries?

Around 1.6 billion people around the world have no electricity. That's 1 600 000 000 people.

Why? First, it costs a fortune to build power stations, and buy the fuels for them. Or to build dams, for hydroelectricity.

And even if you do have power stations and dams, it costs a lot to set up the pylons, and cables, to carry electricity to every rural village.

Many countries just can't afford it.

But with PV cells, you do not need power stations, or pylons, or miles of cable. Every home can make its own electricity. Solar power can transform lives.

Solar power + pedal power. Would you like one of these? ▶

▲ A queue to use a solar-powered mobile phone, in a village in Bangladesh. (At A on the map below.)

▲ Solar power for a yurt (tent) in an isolated spot in Mongolia. (At B on the map below.)

Your turn

1 What is a PV cell? Give its full name, and say (in your own words) what it does.

2 Say whether you think these statements about solar power are true or false. The photos may help.
   A Every home could make its own electricity.
   B You must live near a city to use solar power.
   C Solar power is used only in rich countries.
   D It is not sunny enough in the UK for solar power.
   E Solar power makes global warming worse.
   F You can't make solar power at night.
   G The UK is better in summer, for solar power.

3 What are the three main advantages of solar power, in your opinion? List them in order of importance.

4 Now give any disadvantages you can think of.

5 Look at this map. What does it show?

6 a From the map, which gets the strongest sunshine: Greenland, Spain, or Chad? (Pages 140 - 141?)
   b See if you can explain why.

7 Overall, which *continent* on the map below looks best for solar power?

8 a Solar power has special advantages for poorer countries. Explain why.
   b From what you know about the world already, see if you can name three poorer countries with very strong sunlight, that they could use for energy.

9 You are an inventor. And here's a challenge.
   a Think up a new invention, using PV cells. For example for tourists, or climbers, or mums with toddlers.
   b Draw a labelled sketch of it.
   c Then make up a name and a slogan for it.

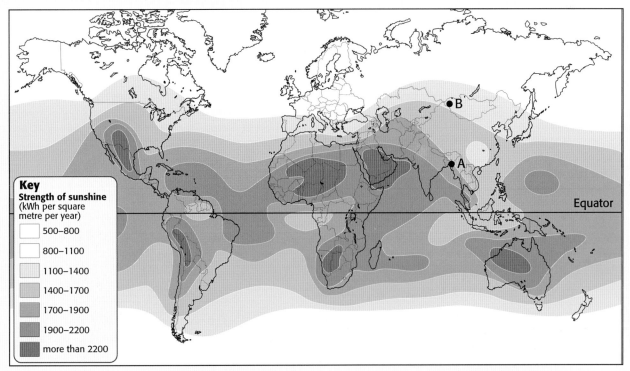

Key
Strength of sunshine
(kWh per square metre per year)

- 500–800
- 800–1100
- 1100–1400
- 1400–1700
- 1700–1900
- 1900–2200
- more than 2200

Equator

Going solar in Gosaba

Here you'll learn how solar power improved life in a rural village in India.

Where's Gosaba ?

This is Debu. He is 15. He lives in Gosaba, on a small island in an area called Sundarbans in India.

His home is the one on the far right above. It has a thatched roof and two rooms.

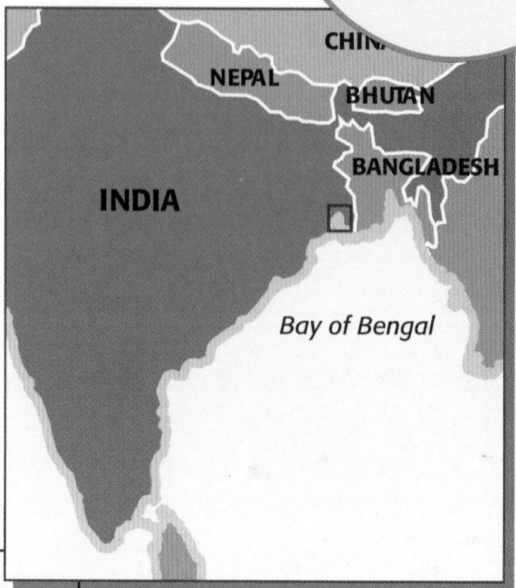

This sketch map shows Sundarbans, with Gosaba marked in.

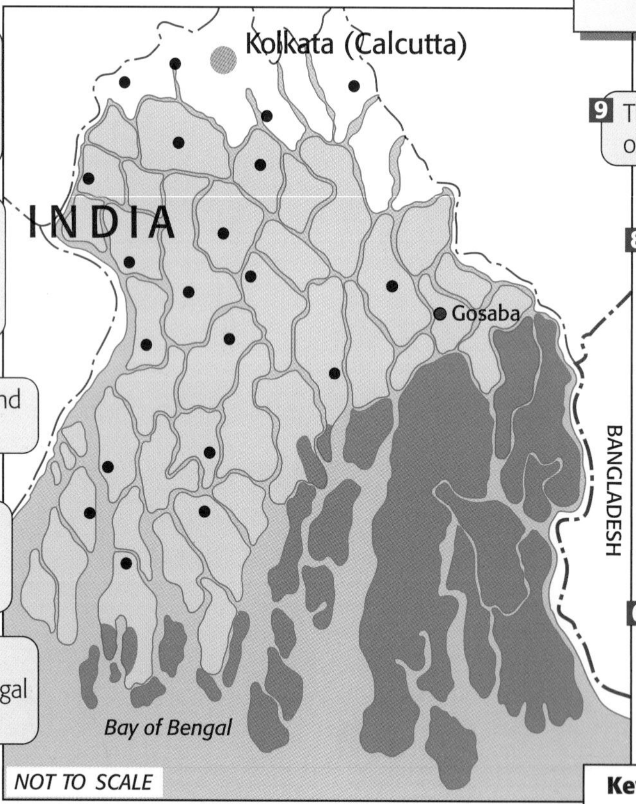

Kolkata (Calcutta)

INDIA

● Gosaba

BANGLADESH

Bay of Bengal

NOT TO SCALE

1 Sundarbans is a **delta** area (like its neighbour Bangladesh). It has 102 islands. This map shows just some of them.

2 Over millions of years, water flowing out from two great rivers, the Ganges and Brahmaputra, deposited sediment in the area.

3 It built up to form the islands – and the water just ran round them.

4 Now the region is teeming with rivers, stream, and canals. Only some rivers are shown here.

5 It also has thick swampy **mangrove forests**. With Bengal tigers, turtles and crocodiles !

9 The only way to get to most of the islands is by boat.

8 Most people live on tiny farms in small hamlets – like Debu. His father also earns some money from fishing.

7 About 200 000 people live in the area shown on this map. 15 000 live on Debu's island.

6 The climate is hot and humid. There are heavy monsoon rains from June to October.

Key
⬤ city
● main town or village of island
  sea/river
  mangrove forest
—-— boundary of Sundarbans
—·—· border with Bangladesh

Where Gosaba got its energy

Before 1997, the people of Gosaba used **kerosene** for lighting and cooking. Kerosene is made from oil. It gives out soot that turns walls and ceilings black, and fumes that irritate your eyes and lungs. It gives a dim light. And it can set the house on fire !

Some homes in Gosaba had TV, running on batteries. But TV batteries don't last long, and cost a lot. That means less money for other things.

Solar power arrives

In 1997, some homes and other buildings in Gosaba got solar power, as a trial. Debu's home was one.

The governments of India and the USA paid for most of the project. But the users also had to pay a little – £23 a year for 5 years.

Solar power has made a big difference to Debu and his family.

In fact the project was a big success. So other parts of the Sundarbans are going solar too. The target is for 31 of the 53 inhabited islands to go solar by 2008.

▲ Up go the PV cells on Debu's roof …

◄ … and on go the lights!

Your turn

1 a In which country is this area of Sundarbans?
  b In which continent is it?
  c Which country is it next to?

2 Explain why:
  a there are so many islands in Sundarbans
  b floods are a problem there.

3 India has a National Grid for electricity, like the UK. Cables carry electricity from power stations to different places. But India will never be able to extend its grid to Gosaba. Suggest reasons for this.

4 Before solar power, Debu's family had just two kerosene lamps like this one. They lit them every evening when it got dark, around 6. What problems can kerosene lamps cause?

5 a The table on the right shows the results of a survey in Gosaba. Which was the most common reason people gave, for liking solar power?
  b See if you can explain why this reason is so important to people.

6 Display the results of the survey in any way you like. For example you could draw a pictogram or bar graph. Make it look interesting!

7 It is 1997. You are Debu. Write to your cousin Kali in Kolkata telling her about solar power, and how it has affected your family.

8 'Solar power in Gosaba is a great example of sustainable development.' Do you agree? Explain.

Impact of solar power on people in Gosaba	
Benefit	% who mentioned this
Better light	80
No fumes to irritate the eyes	85
Less coughing	10
Can earn more now since can work longer hours	25
Easier to serve food now	12
Easier to use than kerosene	64
Helps children to study	88
Can watch more TV news	44
Can watch more TV serials and films	78

The big picture

Geography is brilliant. It even covers crime! This chapter is all about crime. These are the big ideas behind the chapter:

◆ Crime affects all of us, not just the victims.

◆ It's easier to commit crimes in some places than others – so criminals think about geography!

◆ Maps are good for showing where crimes occur, and working out why.

◆ Today, when we build new buildings, we try to make them more 'crime proof'.

Your goals for this chapter

By the end of this chapter you should be able to answer these questions:

◆ What do these terms mean?

crime   victim   offender   sentence   secure accommodation

◆ Crime affects all of us – not just the victims. In what ways? (Give at least three.)

◆ What do these terms mean?

fraud   burglary   vandalism   domestic violence

assault   environmental crime   terrorism   crime hotspot

◆ Some crime is *not* reported to the police. Why not? What examples can I give? (At least two.)

◆ The geography and layout of a place can help to make it easier, or harder, to commit crime. What examples can I give? (At least four.)

◆ What kind of things can we do to cut down burglary, theft, and street crime? (Give at least five.)

And then …

When you finish this chapter, come back to this page and see if you have met your goals!

> **Did you know?**
> ◆ There are about 90 000 people in prison in the UK at this moment.

> **Did you know?**
> ◆ There are about 160 prisons in the UK.

> **Did you know?**
> ◆ There are about 9 million people in prison around the world.

> **Did you know?**
> ◆ About 70 countries still put people to death, for some crimes.

> **What if...**
> ◆ ... you got sent to prison for something?

Your chapter starter

Page 98 shows policemen on patrol. They're looking out for crime.

What's a crime?

What kind of crimes could happen in that area?

Who decides what counts as a crime?

Has it got anything to do with you?

But it wasn't me.

A crime story

In this unit you will explore how crime affects more than just the victim.

The offender's story

It happened a year ago when I was 13.

I was walking through the park with my friend and we were talking about things we like. You know, clothes and all. There was a woman in front of us, quite old. My friend said 'I'm going to get her bag'. He ran and grabbed the bag. She held on and screamed. He gave a tug. So did I. She fell back on to the iron railings.

Now she's paralysed. I am sorry about her. I got an 18-month sentence. It wasn't even my idea but they said I was guilty too.

I wish it had never happened. But it did and I can't change it. Now I have a criminal record and the police will always be watching me.

At school they teach you things like cooking, and crossing the road safely, and what to do in a fire. But they never teach you not to steal – not really.

▲ *The offender.*

The victim's story

It has ruined my life. 46 years old, and in a wheelchair.

I had a good job at the hotel. My children were doing well. We were an ordinary family. And then in just a few minutes everything changed. What did I do to deserve this?

The worst part is the effect on my family. It's like a big dark cloud over all of us. We can never have a normal life again.

My husband had to leave his job and take a part-time job to look after me. My children worry all the time. My son has got really depressed. He used to do well at school but now he's getting bad reports, and he'll probably fail his exams.

I never go out now – I sit out the back in the garden. When my husband wheeled me down the street once, I got panicky. I felt everyone was staring at me.

Those two boys just got a few years between them. I got a life sentence.

So – who pays the penalty?

In this sad story, the offenders were punished for their crime. The victim was punished too. But they were not the only ones who suffered, as you'll see next.

▲ *The victim.*

Paying for crime

90 km

Key

The victim and her family

⊙ The victim and her family live here.

◯ This is the park where the crime took place.

● The victim had to have several serious and expensive operations in this hospital.

The offenders and their families

● The secure accommodation where the two boys are being held. They are not allowed out.

● The families of the two boys live in these houses. Their neighbours won't talk to them now.

Other people

● Five people in these houses need operations. But the hospital had to delay them in order to treat the victim. (It ran short of money.)

● Eleven people in these houses used to walk in the park. Not any more. They are too afraid.

● The owner of this house was about to sell it – but the crime put the buyers off.

● The police and prisons cost a lot to run. The money comes from taxes …

◯ … so everyone who pays taxes pays more because of crime.

Your turn

1 Why do you think the boy wanted the bag?

2 Who suffered because of this crime? Make a list.

3 The boy who snatched the bag was 11. He got an 18-month sentence too. Do you think it was fair that:
 a both boys got the same sentence?
 b they got 18 months?

4 Write down the meaning of each term. (Glossary?)
 victim   offender   sentence
 secure accommodation

5 We all pay for crimes other people commit. You pay every time you go shopping! Look at this:

**Theft from UK shops costs
£ billions every year!**

To see how you pay for shop theft, write these sentences in the correct order.

A The shop has to find money to pay for the stolen goods, and the security staff.

B So the shop hires security staff to stop theft.

C Shoplifters steal things from a shop.

D So you pay more when you go shopping.

E So it charges more for the things it sells.

6 Mugging and shoplifting are crimes. So is dumping poisonous chemicals in rivers. Which do you think is the best definition of a crime?
 a An action that harms a person.
 b An action that breaks the law.
 c An action that offends people.

Different kinds of crime

In this unit you'll explore and compare different kinds of crime.

It's a bad bad day in the city …

1 In a pub, a man is selling new laptops. Only £80 each. (His mate stole them from a truck.)

6 Two boys are spraying graffiti on the railway bridge.

13 In a secret room, three people are working hard, printing fake £5 notes.

7 On the 2.30 train, nine people are travelling without a ticket.

8 In a café, a man of 40 waits for a young girl he contacted on the internet. (He told her he was 15.)

2 Three cars on this street are parked on double yellow lines.

14 At a corner, one young man is stabbing another to death, because of the colour of his ski.

3 A young woman is buying a coat on the internet, using a stolen credit card.

9 The head office of a company. Fumes from its factories around the UK are damaging people's lungs.

15 A man parks a car outside the embassy. The bomb in it will go off in 15 minutes.

4 A husband has just beaten his wife up again. Her face is bruised and bleeding.

10 A stranger is climbing in a window, and will steal some jewellery.

16 Two masked men have just walked into the shop. One aims a gun at the staff while the other lifts cash from the tills.

11 In the school, three girls are bullying another girl. They slap and kick at her.

17 An older boy grips a 12-year-old in a headlock, and takes his mobile phone.

5 Three people in here are watching TV. No TV licence.

12 A boy has just broken into a battered old car and is driving it away.

18 In a corner shop, the shopkeeper is selling cigarettes to a girl of 13.

How much crime is there in the UK?

The UK has quite a lot of crime. (Most is not very serious.) But not all of it gets reported to the police, or recorded by them.

So every year the government carries out its own survey. Households in England and Wales are asked about crimes they suffered over the past twelve months.

The survey shows many more crimes than the police records do – in fact over three times as many!

This table shows the results for one year. The numbers are all in thousands. So there were 6660 thousand (or over six million) thefts in England and Wales that year.

But the survey does not ask about crimes like fraud or drug dealing. So you need to look at police records too, to get a better picture.

British Crime Survey: one year's results

Type of crime		Number of times committed (thousands)
1 Vandalism		2465
2 Thefts	burglary	943
	of or from cars	2121
	of bicycles	370
	other household thefts	1283
	thefts from people	622
	other thefts of personal property	1321
	Total	6660
3 Violent crimes	mugging (to rob)	283
	wounding (in fights)	655
	common assault (hitting)	1654
	Total	2592
Total of all crimes		**11 717**

Your turn

1 All the events given on the photo are crimes.
See if you can pick a number from the photo to match each term below. (A different number for each.)

  a murder   b forgery
  c vandalism   d armed robbery
  e burglary   f domestic violence
  g fraud   h handling stolen goods
  i a traffic offence j environmental crime
  k terrorism   l common assault
  m car theft   n mugging

If you get stuck the glossary may help.

2 Both young people and adults commit crime.
Look at the list of crimes a – n above. Pick out:

  a one that's more likely to be carried out by younger people (under 16) than older people
  b five that are more likely to be carried out by adults
  c two you think just as likely for either group.

3 Young people are often victims of crime. From the *photo*, pick out five situations where the victims are always, or often, young people.

4 All the crimes on the photo took place in a city. But some of them could take place in a rural area. Give the numbers for four crimes that:

  a could easily take place in a tiny rural hamlet
  b are unlikely to take place in a rural area.

5 Many crimes are not reported to the police.
Suggest a reason why these crimes from the photo were not reported.

  a 12   b 4   c 18   d 11

6 Look at the table above.
  a How many crimes did the survey find altogether? (Check the heading of the last column!)
  b Of the three main types of crime, which one was the most common?
  c There were about two and a half million acts of vandalism. Give four examples of vandalism.
  d Which type of theft was the most common? Suggest reasons.
  e Which type of theft was the least common? Suggest reasons.

7 All crime is wrong. But some crimes are more serious than others.
  a Draw a scale like the one below. Make it the width of your page, and divide it into three equal parts. Label the divisions.

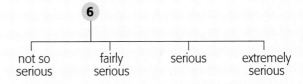

not so serious   fairly serious   serious   extremely serious

  b Now mark in these crimes from the photo on your scale, where you think they should go:

    1   2   7   8   9   15

    Crime 6 has been put on the scale as an example.
  c In b, how did you decide on the *most* serious and *least* serious crimes? Explain your thinking.

Did you know?
◆ Murder is quite rare compared with other crimes.
◆ There are about 13 000 times more thefts than murders!

Criminal geography!

In this unit you'll explore the links between location and crime. And find out who's most likely to get burgled!

The criminal's mental map

We all have **mental maps** (maps in our mind) of areas we know well. Look at this mental map for a criminal.

The criminal will head for areas:
- that he knows well
- that offer opportunities for crime
- where he can get away without being seen.

This criminal has three areas to target – near home, near work, and near where he goes for shopping and entertainment.

And now it's time to go exploring!

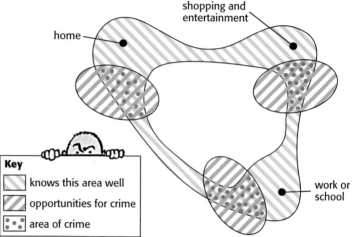

Key

	knows this area well
	opportunities for crime
	area of crime

Your turn

First, put yourself in a criminal's shoes.

1 You are a house burglar. You know all the places in the photos on the opposite page.
  a Which two places would you target?
  b For each, give reasons for your choice.

2 What kinds of crimes might occur in the places shown in these photos? Give reasons for your answers.

  a **4** b **5** c **6** d **7** e **8** f **9**

Now, be yourself.

3 In which place in the photos would you feel safest, walking around by yourself:
  a during the day? b at night?
  Give the numbers of the photos, and your reasons.

4 In which place would you feel least safe, walking around by yourself:
  a during the day? b at night?
  Again give the photo numbers, and your reasons.

Next, you are a crime prevention officer.

5 Choose one photo from page 105 with people in. What advice would you give those people about protecting themselves from crime, in that situation?

6 If a place shows **physical disorder** it means it looks run-down and messy.
  a Which photo do you think shows highest physical disorder?
  b Do you think there's a link between physical disorder, and risk of crime? How could you check?

And finally, think about being burgled.

7 The table below shows the risk of burglary. 3.4% of households in rural areas are likely to be burgled, and 5.6% of all households.

The risk of household burglary	%
Head of household aged 16–24	15.2
Living in an area of high physical disorder	12.0
Living in rented property	9.7
Living in the inner city	8.5
Living in a council estate	8.1
Living in a flat	7.2
On a main road	6.6
Average risk of being burgled	5.6
Earning more than £30 000 a year	5.0
Living in property they own	4.2
Living in a detached house	4.1
Head of household 65 or older	3.8
Living in rural areas	3.4

Draw a bar graph to show the data in the table. It will be a wide graph, so you can turn your page sideways. Start like this:

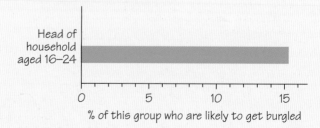

8 Now it's time to analyse the data in your bar graph. The text on the opposite page will help. This clue box might help too !

Suggest reasons why the risk of being burgled is:

a lowest in rural areas

b low for people aged over 65

c lower if you own your home than if you rent it

d above average if you live on a main road

e below average if you earn more than £30 000

f higher for flats than for detached houses

g highest where the head of the household is aged 16–24.

CLUE BOX

Not everyone can afford burglar alarms and good locks.

Lots of us don't know our neighbours.

In busy places nobody pays much attention to strangers.

Burglars prefer places with no-one at home.

We take more care of places we own.

If you own lots of things you might fit a burglar alarm, and good door and window locks.

In this unit you'll explore crime spots, using a map and an aerial photo.

Put your police hat on !

You are in charge of crime control for the area on the map below.
The matching photo on page 107 will help you answer these questions.

Evening all.

Your turn

1 There were several fights along one part of
  the High Street, in the last six months.
  a Suggest a reason for this. (Check building use?)
  b What could you do to prevent trouble here?
    Come up with some suggestions.
    Then put them in order, with the best one first.

2 Now look at square 1436.
  a What was the main crime here?
  b Suggest a reason for this. (Check the photo.)
  c What will you do to prevent this crime?
    Put your suggestions in order, best one first.

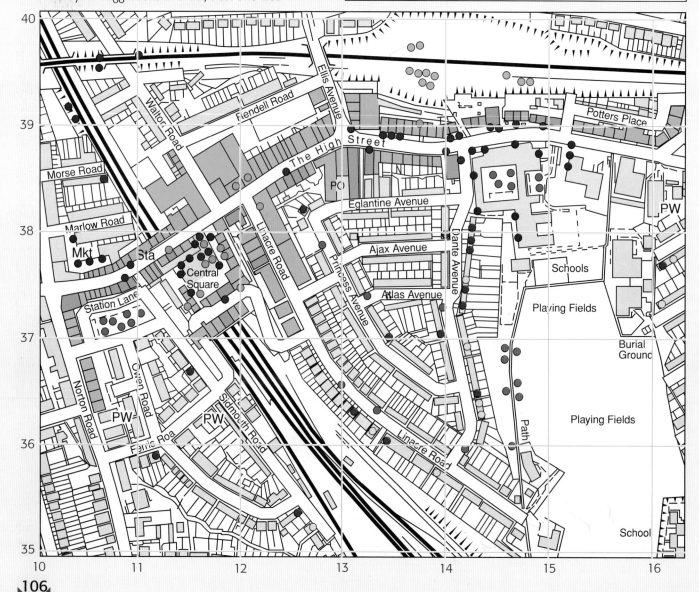

Key

railway and railway bridges

ⲧⲧⲧⲧ embankment

Businesses

shops (all types)

financial centres (banks,
building societies, post office)

places of entertainment (pubs,
clubs, wine bars, cafes, restaurants)

Abbreviations

PW   place of worship
PO   post office
Mkt market
Sta station

Crime over last 6 months

● household burglary
○ repeat household burglary
● break-ins to businesses
● assault (fighting)
● theft of or from cars
○ illegal dumping of rubbish
● vandalism
● mugging

0   600 m

3 Yesterday two of your police team visited each house on the right of Dante Avenue (going north). They offered to write the postcode on valuable things like computers, with a special invisible ink.
   a What is a *postcode*?
   b Why did they want to write it on things?
   c Why did they choose this road?

4 Houses on the left of Dante Avenue are burgled far less often than those on the right. Suggest a reason.

5 Say which two grid squares were worst for this crime, and give reasons:
   a theft of or from cars
   b illegal dumping of rubbish

6 Vandalism is a problem too. Windows broken, phone boxes smashed, and walls sprayed with graffiti. It is a special problem in squares 1438 and 1137. Suggest reasons for this.

7 A **crime hotspot** has more crime than the other places around it. Where is the main crime hotspot in the map area? Try to give reasons for this.

8 Mr Williams rang to say he has now been burgled 6 times in 6 months. He lives where the yellow dot is, in square 1235. The photo below shows his house.
   a Suggest reasons why his house is burgled so often. Look at the map *and* the photos.
   b Now write to Mr Williams with some advice about how he could stop his house being burgled.

In the fight against crime

In this unit you'll learn about things we can do to deter criminals.

Protecting property

Criminals like an easy target – and not to get caught. So we can make their lives more difficult. Here are some ways to protect property ...

1 Make the target harder to get at. This is called **target hardening**. You could put in high fences, window bars, and strong locks.

2 Make it easier to spot that a crime is being committed. You could fit burglar alarms and bright lights, and hire security guards.

3 Make it easy to track a stolen item. For example, fit a car with a hidden device that uses **GPS**, so that you can always tell where it is.

A GPS, or **global positioning system**, makes use of 27 satellites that circle the Earth twice a day, over 19 000 km above us.

Designing out crime

The **built environment** means all the built things around us – houses, streets, shopping centres and so on. As you have seen, it can give lots of opportunities for crime.

Now people think about crime before they build something new. They try to design it to prevent crime.

It is called **designing out crime**. Look at this new housing estate.

Nah!

> Target hardening is built in.
> ◆ All windows have locks, and glass that's very hard to break.
> ◆ The outer doors are strong, with strong locks.
> ◆ Every house has a burglar alarm.

> The layout makes crime easier to spot.
> ◆ People can easily keep an eye on each other's homes and cars.
> ◆ There's only one way in and out of the estate. So burglars can't escape easily.
> ◆ All paths are out in the open, easy to see from the houses.

A space to watch over

The estate above has a **defensible space** around it. That means a space people can watch over and protect. There are no hidden alleys or corners. People can see if strangers are trying to break into houses, or steal cars.

Space like this, that people can watch over, is a good way to fight crime.

Today, the police are happy to check plans for new estates, and other developments, to make sure they are anti-crime. They will even suggest which doors, windows, and locks to use.

Your turn

1 What does *target hardening* mean?

2 a First, make a larger copy of this Venn diagram.

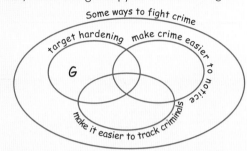

Some ways to fight crime

target hardening   make crime easier to notice

G

make it easier to track criminals

b Now look at the list below. In which loop of your Venn diagram should each item go? Mark its letter in. (One is done already.) If you think an item belongs to more than one loop, put the letter where they overlap.

A a lock for your bicycle
B a bullet-proof vest
C a 'krooklok' for a car steering wheel
D a CCTV camera (like the one shown on the right)
E security tags on clothes in a shop
F a guard dog
G a high wall with metal spikes on top
H a shatterproof glass screen in the post office
I a Neighbourhood Watch scheme (Glossary!)
J a special mobile phone for children, that uses GPS
K a bodyguard

3 CCTV (or closed circuit TV) is used in shops and on streets. Some years ago, CCTV cameras were installed in the town centre in Airdrie in Scotland. Look at this table.

Airdrie

| | In the 12 months … | |
	before CCTV	after CCTV
Car break-ins	480	20
Theft of cars	185	13
Serious assaults	39	22
Vandalism	207	36
Break-ins to business premises	263	15

a Overall, did CCTV reduce the number of crimes?
b Which type of crime did it reduce most?
c Which did it reduce least? Try to give a reason.

4 You are (still) in charge of crime for the area on page 106. You have money for just two CCTV cameras. Below is a list of grid references.
From this list, pick out the two best places for your CCTV cameras, and give your reasons.

a 145365   b 138375   c 113374
d 139389   e 145385   f 115382

5 What do these terms mean?
   a designing out crime   b defensible space
   Answer in your own words, using the last photo on page 108 to help you.

6 The methods in this unit help to reduce crime. But they don't stop it altogether! Look at these opinions:

If you want to cut crime, give young people interesting things to do.

To really cut crime we must teach people that it's wrong.

To get rid of crime – just get rid of poverty.

I think the best way to cut crime is to punish criminals very severely.

a Choose any *two* of the four opinions.
b For each, decide whether you agree or not. Then write down what you will say to that person in reply.

… and now some even shout at you!

A CCTV camera can turn, tilt, and zoom …

8 Oi Brazil !

Welcome to Brazil! The fifth largest country in the world, with the fifth largest population. Where you'll find …

▲ … the world's best carnivals …

▲ … the world's largest rainforest, full of exotic plants and animals …

▲ … huge cities …

▲ … glorious sandy beaches …

60°

Equator

SOUTH AMERICA

Tropic of Capricorn

BRAZIL

▲ … great poverty …

▲ … great wealth …

▲ … people of every race and colour …

▲ … and stunning scenery.

The big picture

This chapter is all about Brazil. These are the big ideas behind the chapter:

◆ Brazil is a large country, rich in natural resources.

◆ It is a country of big contrasts (in climate, wealth, and so on).

◆ It is developing quite quickly.

◆ But it still has a lot of poverty – and a very unequal society.

◆ Brazil's rainforest has been disappearing fast.

Your goals for this chapter

By the end of this chapter you should be able to answer these questions:

◆ Where in the world is Brazil?

◆ What can I say about these, and where are they on the map?

Brazil's main physical features   its climate zones   its ecosystems

◆ What kinds of natural resources does Brazil have?

◆ Why does Brazil have such a big mixture of races?

◆ Which parts of Brazil are most crowded? And most empty? Why?

◆ Which are Brazil's top 10 cities, and where are they on the map?

◆ What are favelas? Where would I find them? What are they like?

◆ What clues can I look for, to see how developed a country is?

◆ What do these terms mean?

GDP   GDP per capita   life expectancy   infant mortality
adult literacy rate   undernourished

◆ How developed is Brazil, compared to countries like the UK, and India?

◆ Brazil has great *inequality*. What does that mean?

◆ Why is Brazil's rainforest disappearing?

◆ The rainforest could be at greater risk, as Brazil develops. Why?

And then …

When you finish this chapter, come back to this page and see if you have met your goals!

Brazil at a glance
Area: 8.5 million sq km
    (5th largest country in the world)
Population: about 187 million
    (5th largest in the world)
How developed is it?
Ranks about 70th in the world

Did you know?
◆ Oi means Hi in Portuguese ….
◆ … which is the official language of Brazil.

Did you know?
◆ Brazil will host the World Cup in football in 2014.

Did you know?
By 2006, out of 18 World Cup football finals:
◆ Brazil had won 5 times …
◆ … and been runner-up twice.

What if …
◆ … school took you on a trip to Brazil?

Your chapter starter

The photos on page 110 were taken in Brazil.

Where's Brazil?

From the photos, do you think it would be a good place to live?

What else do you know about Brazil, that the photos don't cover?

Terra do futebal!

What's Brazil like?

In this unit you'll learn about Brazil's main physical features, and its climate zones.

Brazil's physical features

The basin of the River Amazon, and the Brazilian Highlands, are Brazil's two main physical features. (Look at the map below.)

The Brazilian Highlands

- A mix of ancient hills, plateaux (high flat areas) and mountains.
- They rise sharply from the coast, forming a steep slope called the Great Escarpment.
- There's just a narrow strip of land between the escarpment and the Atlantic Ocean.

The River Amazon

- Rises in Peru and flows through Brazil to the Atlantic Ocean.
- The world's second longest river – 6580 km. (The Nile is first.)
- Drains over a third of Brazil, including the rainforest (above).
- Has hundreds of tributaries.

Did you know?
- There is not even one bridge over the Amazon, in its 6580 km journey to the ocean.

The coast has many miles of beautiful sandy beaches.

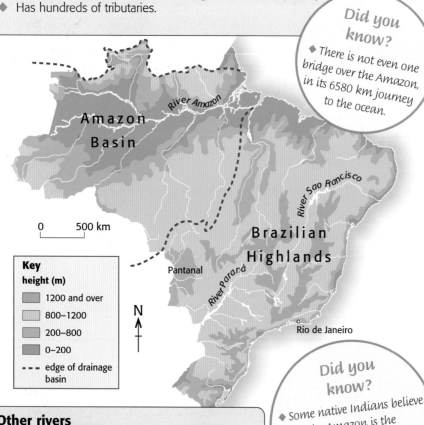

Key
height (m)
- 1200 and over
- 800–1200
- 200–800
- 0–200
- - - edge of drainage basin

N

0   500 km

Amazon Basin

River Amazon

River Sao Francisco

Brazilian Highlands

Pantanal

River Paraná

Rio de Janeiro

Other rivers

- Brazil has a great many rivers. The map above shows just the main ones. Note those names!
- The Paraná is the second longest river in South America (4200 km).

Did you know?
- Some native Indians believe the Amazon is the moon's tears.
- She weeps because she loves the sun but can't get closer to him.

The Sugar Loaf mountain above Rio de Janeiro is made of granite. You can go up it by cable car.

Brazil's climate

Brazil is huge – over four-fifths the size of Europe. And because it is so large, it has a range of climates – just like Europe. Most of it lies in the tropics so is hot all year, with an average temperature of around 25 °C. But rainfall varies, due to factors such as:

◆ the height of the land

◆ the distance from the coast

◆ the prevailing wind direction.

Now look at its climate zones.

hot with very dry season

◆ hot all year, and gets a bit hotter in the dry season

◆ not very much rain in the wet season – and if it fails there is drought.

hot and wet

◆ hot all year – the temperature does not vary much

◆ very wet, with most rain falling in the first half of the year.

a bit cooler, and wet

◆ a bit cooler since it's further from the equator

◆ wet all year, but a bit drier towards the middle of the year.

hot and wet, with dry season

◆ quite hot all year (like a hot summer's day in the UK)

◆ has a wet and dry season

◆ most rain falls in December to March, when the sun is more directly overhead.

milder and wet

◆ has different seasons, like us

◆ some rain all year round

◆ you may even get snow in winter (around July).

Equator

N

prevailing wind

Tropic of Capricorn

0   500 km

Your turn

1 Which are the two main physical features of Brazil?

2 Write down three facts about the Amazon.

3 This is about the climate map above. (Unit 3.9 and the map on page 112 will help you answer it.)

  a It is always cooler at D than at A. Why?

  b It is always cooler at E than at F. Why?

  c Give a reason why it's wetter at F than at B.

  d C is very close to the equator, and to the Amazon. Try to explain why it's always hot *and* wet there.

4 On the right are four climate graphs. Match them to the four places A, B, C and D, on the map above.

5 Copy and complete, using words from the list below:
The _____ _____ of Brazil is _____ and _____ .
The large central area is _____ with a _____ _____.
The _____ is _____ with four seasons like the UK.
The driest part of all is in the _____ _____.
south   hot   north east   wet
milder   dry season   north west

6 A challenge! When it's winter in London it is summer at D. Explain why. Draw diagrams if that helps.

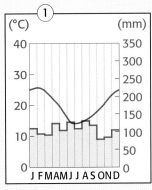

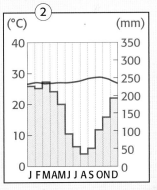

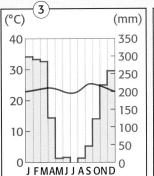

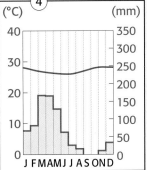

Brazil's natural riches

In this unit you'll learn about Brazil's ecosystems and natural resources.

Brazil's ecosystems

As you saw, Brazil has different climate zones. Which means
it has different ecosystems too. Have you heard of any of these?

The caatinga

- ◆ Semi-arid (like a desert).
- ◆ The plants are mainly shrubs and cacti, with very few trees.
- ◆ Lots of scorpions, spiders, snakes, and colourful birds live here.

The tropical rainforest

- ◆ The largest area of rainforest in the world. It covers about 40 % of Brazil!
- ◆ It grows thick and lush.
- ◆ It teems with plants, animals and insects. (Parrots, monkeys, sloths and orchids just for a start.)

Equator

Did you know?
- ◆ Brazil has over 1600 species of birds.

Tropic of Capricorn

N

The Mata Atlantica

- ◆ 500 years ago there was thick forest along the coast. (*Mata* means forest.)
- ◆ Some was rainforest., with a huge range of trees. Including the brazil trees that gave Brazil its name.
- ◆ But most of it has been cut down. Only about one tenth is left.

The Pantanal

- ◆ The world's largest swampland.
- ◆ It's full of water-loving plants and animals, including giant anaconda (snakes that can swim).

The cerrado

- ◆ This has a wet and dry season.
- ◆ In the dry season the grass gets so dry that lightning sets it on fire.
- ◆ There are not many trees – and they have thick bark to protect them against fire.
- ◆ The animals here include deer, rhea (like ostriches) and wolves.

The pampas

- ◆ These are grassy plains.
- ◆ Now they are heavily farmed, with many cattle ranches.

Brazil's natural resources

Brazil is rich in natural resources. Just look at these:

Sources of energy
◆ Brazil has lots of oil and gas. Huge new oil and gas wells were found in 2007 – around 6 km below the Atlantic Ocean!
◆ It has many big fast-flowing rivers. It has built dams on some, giving 80% of its electricity.

▲ One of Brazil's big dams.

Minerals
◆ Brazil is one of the world's top producers of iron, aluminium, tin, and several other metals …
◆ … and of diamonds and other precious stones …

▲ An iron ore mine in the rainforest.

Timber
◆ Timber has been shipped from Brazil for over 500 years.
◆ Logging for timber is one reason why the rainforest is disappearing.

▲ Logging in the rainforest.

Soil, and climate
◆ Brazil has a wide range of soils, and climates.
◆ So it can grow a wide range of crops: coffee, soya beans, rice, bananas, oranges, cotton …
◆ It grows huge amounts of sugar cane. Much of it goes to make **ethanol**, for use as a fuel in cars.
◆ Animal farming is important too, especially cattle and chickens.

▲ A sugar cane worker.

So Brazil is lucky. Its natural resources are helping to make it wealthy. It is the world's top exporter of coffee, sugar, soya beans, beef, chicken, oranges and orange juice. It is the second largest exporter of iron ore. Soon it will be in the top 10 oil-exporting countries too.

But not all good news

Brazil's rainforest contains many natural resources – and most of it has not even been explored yet. But it is already disappearing very fast: through logging, and clearing land for farming, mining, and building roads. You can find out more about this later in the chapter.

Your turn

1 a What is an ecosystem? (Unit 4.1 will help.)
  b Name six ecosystems in Brazil, and write two sentences about each.
2 Look at the map on page 114.
  a Plants grow really well at **X** on the map. Why?
  b A cactus can store water in its stem. Explain why you will find cacti at **Y**, but not at **Z**. Page 113 may help.
3 Why has most of the Mata Atlantica been cut down? (Clues on pages 116 and 118.)
4 *Soil and climate are natural resources.* Do you agree with that statement? Give reasons.
5 a Now make a grid like the one started on the right, for Brazil's rainforest. Extend it and add *mining*, *dams*, *oil exploration*, and *new roads*.

b Look at our grid. It has an **✗** to show that logging is in conflict with the rainforest ecosystem. It harms it. On your grid, mark **✗** where you think two things are in conflict, **✓** where they benefit each other, and **o** if you think they don't affect each other.
c From your grid, do you agree that Brazil's rainforest is under threat? Explain.
6 You are the President of Brazil. Write a speech for TV, explaining why Brazil has a great future, free of poverty.

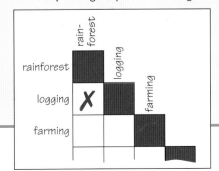

	rain-forest	logging	farming
rainforest			
logging	✗		
farming			

The peopling of Brazil

In this unit you will learn why Brazil has such a great mix of races.

The first people: the Indios

50 000 years ago, the plants and animals had Brazil to themselves. But then at some point – we don't know when – the first humans arrived. They had spread out slowly from East Africa:

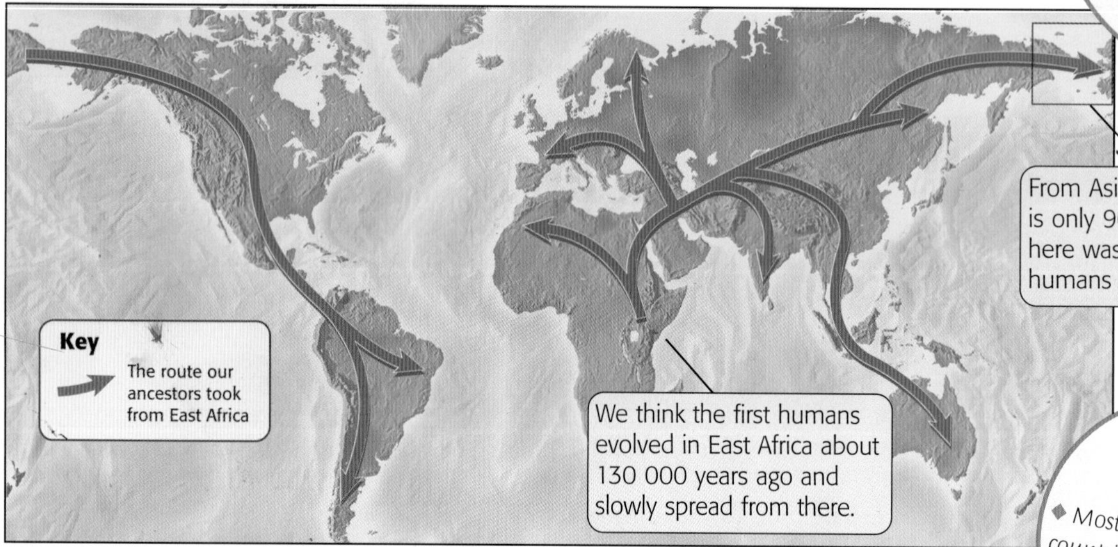
Key
The route our ancestors took from East Africa
From Asia to North America is only 90 km! And the sea here was once ice, so humans just walked across.
We think the first humans evolved in East Africa about 130 000 years ago and slowly spread from there.

By 1500 there were perhaps 5 million people in Brazil. They were called Indians or Indios – by mistake. Because when Christopher Columbus first reached South America, he thought it was India.

Brazil becomes a colony

On 22 April 1500, a fleet of Portuguese sailing ships arrived at the coast of Brazil. They were led by a nobleman named Pedro Alvarez Cabral. He claimed the land for Portugal. It would remain a colony until 1822.

At first, the Portuguese exported brazilwood from the coastal forests in their new colony. Then they switched to sugar cane, which grew well in the warm damp climate along the coast. (Europe was mad about sugar.)

The slave trade begins

Cutting sugar cane is hard work. At first, Indios were forced to work on the sugar plantations. But they rebelled. Then the Portuguese had another idea. They would 'buy' people in Africa, in exchange for cheap goods, and ship them to Brazil to work. It was the start of Europe's **slave trade**.

In 1538 the first slaves arrived. Over the next 300 years, at least 4 million African slaves were taken to Brazil. They were forced to work without pay, and treated like animals. Many more died at sea, in the filthy crowded ships. But at last, in 1888, slavery was abolished in Brazil.

The fortune hunters

By 1700, Brazil's sugar cane industry had begun to decline. And then – gold and diamonds were found. Half a million more Portuguese arrived, hoping to make their fortune. The slaves were put to work in the mines.

Did you know?

- Brazil trees grow in the rainforest – and give us brazil nuts.
- They can grow up to 45 m tall, and live for over 500 years.

Did you know?

- Most Western European countries were involved in the slave trade – including Britain.

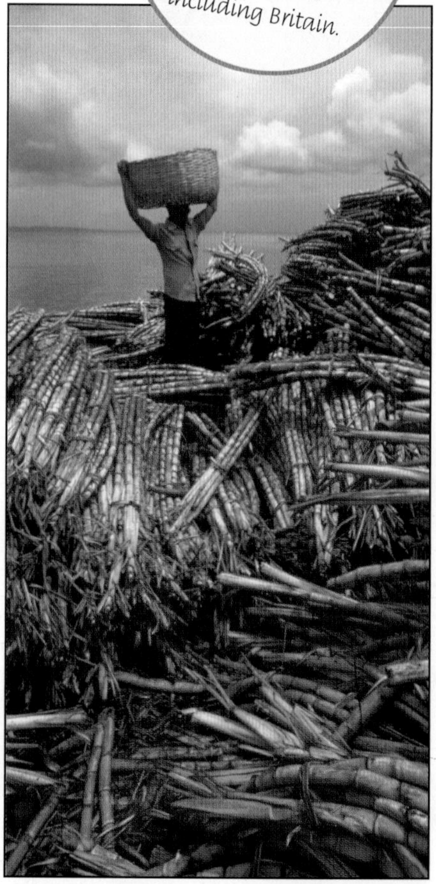

▲ *The sugar cane harvest.*

Workers from Europe

When slavery ended, Brazil took in workers from Europe. This table shows just the largest groups who came. Most worked on the land. But as towns and cities grew and spread, more workers of all kinds were needed. Like builders, doctors, teachers, engineers, cooks …

Today you'll find people of every race, in Brazil.

Immigrants to Brazil, 1876–1976	
Italians	1 600 000
Portuguese	1 500 000
Spanish	600 000
German	300 000
Japanese	250 000

▲ At a football match in multiracial Brazil.

Did you know?
♦ After independence, Brazil had an emperor.
♦ Now it's a republic. (No royal family.)

Your turn

1 Explain each of these facts.
  a About 40% of Brazilians are of African descent.
  b Brazil is a multicultural society. (Glossary?)

2 Look how Brazil's population has grown:

Year	Brazil's population (millions)
1872	10
1900	17
1940	41
1950	52
1960	70
1970	93
1980	121
1991	147
2000	173
2020	?

  a Show this data as a line graph. Use a full page, and continue the *Year* axis up to 2020.
  b From your graph:
   i What was the population in 1960?
   ii By about which year had this figure doubled?
   iii How many years did it take to double?
  c Using your graph, see if you can predict Brazil's population by 2020. Then explain how you did it.

3 Brazil's population rise means it needs more schools. What else does it need more of? Give your answer as a spider map, like the one started here.

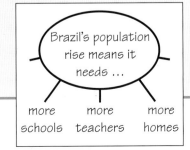

Brazil's population rise means it needs …

more schools   more teachers   more homes

4 A **population pyramid** is a special bar chart that shows ages. Look at this population pyramid for Brazil, for the year 2000. It shows that males aged 10–14 formed nearly 5% of the population.

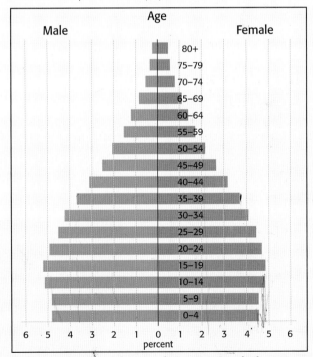

  a About what % of the population consisted of:
   i girls aged 10–14?   ii men aged 35–39?
   iii women aged 50–54?   iv children up to age 4?
  b Overall, which was the largest age group?

5 'Brazil is a country of young people.' Do you agree? Give evidence to back up your answer.

So where is everyone?

Here you'll see how Brazil's population is spread around the country.

Population distribution

About 187 million people live in Brazil. This map shows how they are spread around.

Some areas are highly populated. Some are almost empty.

Look at the main cities.
Rio de Janeiro is the most famous. But São Paolo is Brazil's largest city. Brasilia is the capital. It was built as a new city and 'opened' in 1960.

The table shows the populations of the ten largest cities.

In fact, most of these cities have spread out to join other towns and cities, giving huge **agglomerations**.

The São Paolo agglomeration has over 19 million people !

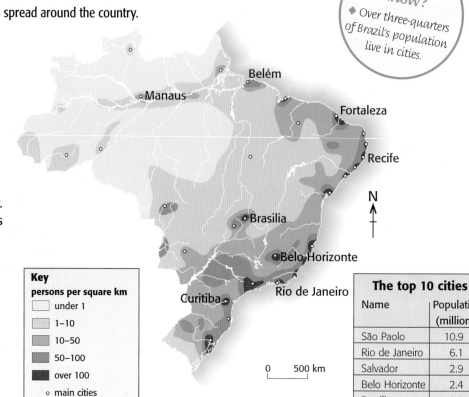

Key
persons per square km
	under 1
	1–10
	10–50
	50–100
	over 100
○	main cities

0   500 km

The top 10 cities	
Name	Population (millions)
São Paolo	10.9
Rio de Janeiro	6.1
Salvador	2.9
Belo Horizonte	2.4
Brasilia	2.5
Fortaleza	2.4
Curitiba	1.8
Manaus	1.7
Recife	1.5
Belém	1.4

The cities are growing fast

Brazil's cities are growing fast. Because people are living longer. And many Brazilians have large families. But most of all, because lots of people from rural areas are moving to them. For reasons like these …

Why is the South East so crowded?

People are always on the move, in Brazil. Usually to find work, and improve their lives.

This map shows Brazil's five regions. Over the years, the biggest flow of people has been to the South East region. Check the boxes to see why.

Key
- ⌒ region boundary
- ⌒ state boundary (each region is made up of states)

N ↑

North

It is mainly rainforest.
- ◆ It has 15 million people. That's 4 people per sq km, on average.
- ◆ They earn £3000 a year on average.
- ◆ Most work in mining, timber, cattle ranching, and farming.
- ◆ 26 out of every 1000 babies here die before their first birthday.

North East

- ◆ 52 million people – or 34 people per sq km, on average.
- ◆ Average earnings: £2250 a year.
- ◆ Some factories.
- ◆ Some good farmland, but drought is a big problem.
- ◆ 37 out of every 1000 babies here die before their first birthday.

Centre West

- ◆ 13 million people – or 9 people per sq km, on average.
- ◆ Average earnings: £6000 a year.
- ◆ Big on soya bean farming, and cattle.
- ◆ Brasilia, the capital city, is here.
- ◆ 20 out of every 1000 babies here die before their first birthday.

South

- ◆ 27 million people – or 50 people per sq km, on average.
- ◆ Average earnings: £5500 a year.
- ◆ Quite a lot of factories.
- ◆ Big on cattle, and growing fruit.
- ◆ 17 out of every 1000 babies here die before their first birthday.

South East

- ◆ 80 million people – or 87 people per sq km, on average.
- ◆ Average earnings: £6300 a year.
- ◆ Lots of factories.
- ◆ Good farmland; it's the main region for sugar cane and coffee.
- ◆ 18 out of every 1000 babies here die before their first birthday.

Your turn

1 Copy and complete these sentences using words or phrases from the box below. (Check the map!)
   a The ____ ____ of Brazil is the most crowded part.
   b Most Brazilians live on or near the ____.
   c Overall, the rainforest area has ____ ____ people.
   d The centre of Brazil is quite ____ populated.
   e The area around São Paolo is ____ populated.
   f São Paolo is Brazil's ____ city and Rio de Janeiro is ____.

   > sparsely   lots of   smallest   very few   second
   > north west   south east   densely   coast   largest

2 Suggest reasons why most Brazilians live on or near the coast. (Think about Brazil's history? And relief?)

3 a Look at the table on the right. Compared with the UK:
   i about many times larger is Brazil, in area?
   ii about how many times larger is its population?
   b Work out the population density for each country.

4 Today the city of São Paolo has twice as many people as 40 years ago. Give some reasons for this.

5 a Use the glossary to find out what these are:
   i push factors   ii pull factors
   b From the speech bubbles on page 118, write a list of:
   i push factors   ii pull factors
   that make people move from rural areas to cities.
   c See if you can think of any other push and pull factors to add to your lists.

6 Look at the boxes above. Which of Brazil's regions:
   a is the most crowded?   b has most factories?
   c is best for earnings?   d is worst for earnings?

7 a In the UK, 5 out of every 1000 babies die before age one. In Brazil, the numbers are higher. See if you can think up reasons. (Could *not enough doctors* be one?)
   b Which is the worst region in Brazil, for baby deaths?

8 Now write a paragraph to explain why lots of people have moved from the North East to the South East region, over the years. The boxes above will help you.

	Brazil	UK
Area (sq km)	8.5 million	0.24 million
Population	187 million	61 million
Population density (number of people per sq km)	?	?

Life in the favela

Here you'll learn what favelas are, and what it's like to live in one.

Luiz moves south

Luiz got off the bus, tired and hungry. It was nearly 30 hours since he had waved goodbye to his mum in his village in Bahia (North East region).

He looked around. His cousin Felipe had promised to wait under a big sign with a hamburger on, outside the bus station. And there he was, all smiles.

Luiz could hardly keep up with him. They hurried along narrow alleys that twisted and turned. It was getting dark. There was music everywhere, and talking, and laughter. Dogs barked, babies cried, TVs blared. Bare-footed children played on the street. Women sat on doorsteps, cooking on charcoal stoves. 'Be careful', said Felipe, as they crossed a gutter filled with sewage.

And then they were home. A shack of brick, and corrugated iron, and wood, and plastic. They went in the open door. And there was Maria and the baby, and hugs and kisses, and a big pot of his favourite stew.

Luiz did not sleep much. The floor was hard, and he was too excited. At dawn, he crept out to look around. Over there were the tall buildings, where Felipe said the rich people lived. Maybe he'd find work there. Gardening, or painting, or building, or even cleaning. And *then* he could build a house of his own.

And so started Luiz's first day, in the Morumbi favela in São Paolo.

▲ Homes in the Morumbi favela.

▼ The Morumbi favela, in São Paolo.

What is a favela?

A favela is a collection of shacks built on waste ground, without permission. It's where the poorest people live.

◆ Most of the people came from rural areas, looking for work.

◆ The shacks are built from anything – including cardboard. When you want a bigger house, you just add a bit more on.

◆ Most do not have legal water or electricity. But most are hooked up illegally, to cables and water mains. (So at busy times the lights go out, and the taps run dry.)

◆ There is no sewage system, and rubbish is not collected. So sewage and rubbish go into open drains.

◆ But you might find little shops, and cafes, and places to get a hair-cut.

◆ People get work wherever they can in the city – in factories, or on building sites, or as servants in the rich people's homes.

◆ Not many favela children finish school. They work, or beg, instead.

◆ There's a high level of violence, drug use, and murder, in the favelas. Some favelas are ruled by gangs.

All of Brazil's cities have favelas. Rio de Janeiro and São Paolo have most. About 1 in 5 people in those two cities live in favelas.

▲ All connected – illegally.

What is being done about them?

The government has tried different approaches to favelas.

◆ Some shacks in São Paolo were knocked down, and low-cost, high-rise flats were built in their place. Look at the photo on the right.

But it was not a success. People felt cut off from life in the favela. They could not extend their homes when they wanted. They could not keep goats or hens in the flats. (Some tried!)

◆ Today the approach is to **upgrade** the favelas. Like this:
   – The residents say what they need. They take part in all decisions.
   – The government pays for improving the **infrastructure**: electricity and water supplies, a sewage system, paths, and roads.
   – The residents can get money for materials (like bricks and cement) to improve their homes.

Upgrading has been a big success. But progress is very very slow.

▲ High-rise flats (in the middle of the photo), built in a favela in São Paolo.

They should bring the bulldozers in and clear that favela away.

Your turn

1 What is a favela? How do you think favelas started?

2 Why do you think Luiz came to São Paolo?

3 What do you think could be good, about life in a favela? Anything?

4 What are the bad things about favelas? List them in order, with what you think is the worst thing first.

5 On day two, Luiz phones his mum. Make up a conversation between them about his new place.

6 This person lives in the wealthy flats looking over the Morumbi favela. What will you say to him in reply?

How developed is Brazil?

Here you will learn what 'developed' means, and how we measure development. Then you will explore some data, to see how developed Brazil is.

What does 'developed' mean?

Some countries are **highly developed**. That means their people have a good standard of living.

Look at this list. It shows things you are likely to find in a highly developed country.

A *less developed* country won't have all those things. For example it may have some good roads – but a lot of dirt tracks. And very few good hospitals.

Every country in the world is at a different stage of development. Some are *more developed* than others. Some have a long way to go.

> **A highly developed country is likely to have …**
> - good roads, railways, airports, phone systems
> - electricity and piped water in all homes
> - good hospitals and schools for everyone
> - lots of other services (shops, cinemas, gyms …)
> - modern factories, and many other businesses
> - enough food for everyone
> - opportunity for everyone to work, and earn a living
> - little or no poverty.

So what about Brazil?

If you travel around Brazil, you'll find some really posh places and people – and some very very poor ones.

To get an idea of how developed it is, overall, you need ways to measure development. Then you can compare Brazil with other countries.

One way is to add up the value of all the goods and services a country produces in a year. Then divide that by the population.

Look at this:

> **Did you know?**
> - In Brazil, the richest 10% of the population is 50 times richer than the poorest 10%.

So the GDP per capita is PPP US$ 9700.

It's what we'd get if the GDP were shared out equally.

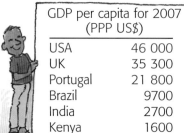

GDP per capita for 2007 (PPP US$)	
USA	46 000
UK	35 300
Portugal	21 800
Brazil	9700
India	2700
Kenya	1600

Look how much it varies

The total value of the goods and services for the year is called the **gross domestic product**, or **GDP**. Think of it as the wealth the country produced that year.

When you divide the GDP by the population, you get the **GDP per capita**. It gives you an idea how well off people are, on average. For Brazil in 2007, it was $9700.

Now compare the GDP per capita for Brazil and other countries. (They are all given in PPP US dollars, to make it easy to compare them.)

Usually, **the higher the GDP per capita, the more developed a country is**. So look at the list above. Which seems more developed, Brazil or the UK?

But GDP per capita does not tell the full story. It does not say what the country produces. Does it produce lots of guns – but not enough food? And it does not say if the wealth is divided fairly.

So we need other ways to measure development too, that look at people's well-being. You will meet some of them in 'Your turn'.

> **What does PPP mean?**
> A US dollar will buy you more in Brazil than in the USA – because things cost less in Brazil.
> PPP means that the GDP per capita figure takes account of this. (PPP stands for *purchasing power parity*.)

Brazil is developing quite fast

People in Brazil are not as well off as people in the UK, or many other countries. Out of 180 countries, Brazil ranks about 70th for GDP per capita. But it is developing quite fast.

The table on the right shows that its GDP per capita keeps on growing. These are the main reasons:

◆ It is earning more and more from crops it sells to other countries.

◆ Once it had to import things like cars, planes, and machinery. These cost a lot. Now it has factories to make them – and it sells them to other countries. It even makes and sells submarines.

◆ Brazil still buys lots of things from other countries. But it sells more than it buys. So, overall, it makes money from its trading.

Soon it will do even better. It will earn a fortune by selling oil from that huge new oil well off the coast, discovered in 2007.

But it still has problems

In spite of all the money it earns, Brazil has about 38 million very poor people – or 1 in 5 of the population. That's because its wealth is very unequally shared. You can find out more about this in the next unit.

GDP per capita for Brazil	
Year	GDP per capita (PPP US$)
1975	5500
1990	6400
1995	6900
2000	7200
2005	8600
2007	9700

▲ Another jet nearly ready, in Brazil.

Your turn

1 a What does *GDP* mean?
  b What does *GDP per capita* mean?

2 a GDP per capita is called a **development indicator**. What do you think this term means? See if you can explain in your own words. Then check the glossary.
  b But GDP per capita does not give a full picture of development. Explain why.

3 Some other development indicators are given below. They tell you about the well-being of people in a country.
  a What does *life expectancy* mean?
  b As a country develops, life expectancy rises – people live longer. See if you can explain why. (Some ideas: more money for food? more hospitals? better housing?)

4 Now look at the other three indicators below. For each, say whether it will *rise* or *fall* as the country develops, and give one reason.

5 So, is Brazil growing more developed, less developed, or staying the same? Give evidence from the table below, to support your answer.

Changes in Brazil Indicator	1980	2007
GDP per capita (PPP $US)	6800	9700
Life expectancy (years)	62	72
Infant mortality (number per 1000 babies)	67	28
Adult literacy rate, %	76	89
% undernourished	15	7

Life expectancy	Infant mortality	Adult literacy rate	Undernourished people
How many years a person in that country can expect to live for.	How many babies per thousand born alive who die before they're 1 year old.	% of people aged 15 and over who can read and write a simple sentence.	% of the population who don't get enough to eat, and live in hunger.

Inequality in Brazil

In this unit you will learn about one big challenge Brazil must tackle: the inequality in its society.

Barbra's day

My mum woke me as usual at 6 am – groan. Coconut pancakes and orange juice for breakfast. Then dad's driver drove me to school for 7. We had Miss Cardoso today – boring! When school finished at 12 we had dance class for an hour. We do all kinds of modern dance.

Magaretta's mother drove us home, and we got my mum and my two brothers and went to the beach. We do that two or three times a week. We joined in a game of volleyball for a while, and swam. Magaretta and I read magazines.

After the beach, homework for an hour. Then dad came home from the office and we had dinner. Lucia is our cook and she cooked feijoada today. It's a bean and pork stew.

Now I'm going to watch TV. Then I'll have a bath and go to bed. But first I want mum to promise to take me shopping for clothes tomorrow. It's Saturday, and I need something special for Anita's party.

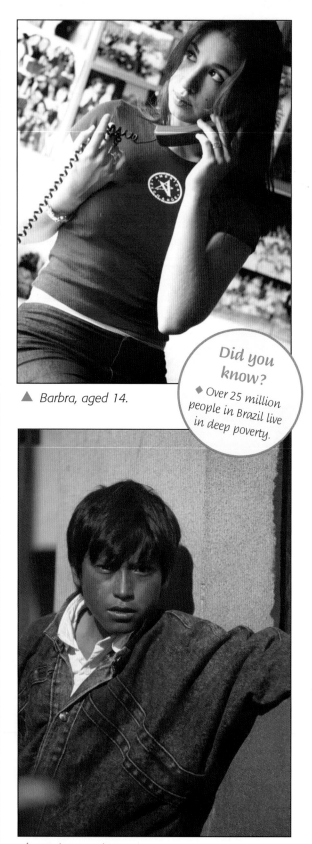

▲ Barbra, aged 14.

Did you know?
◆ Over 25 million people in Brazil live in deep poverty.

Pedro's day

I always wake at 5 am. You can't sleep late in our house – not with all seven of us in one room and the baby crying! I grabbed my bucket and sponge and ran. It's about 3 km to our junction.

Francesco was already there and traffic was busy. So I filled my bucket at the petrol station tap and got started. You have to be fast washing windscreens at the traffic lights – they don't stay on red that long.

Most of the drivers are okay. But some are really nasty –they wait till you finish and then grin and drive off without giving you any money.

At 11 we took a break. We went to the market and bought bread and soup. We ate on the corner as usual. Francesco went on as usual about getting a proper job. He says there are classes to teach poor people like us about computers, and we should try to get into one. But we can't even read!

We'll stay at the junction until it's dark and most people have gone home from work. Then I'll run home really fast. I'm always afraid a favela gang will attack me and take my money. Or else I'll fall into a drain and ruin my jeans.

I make about 8 reals a day. (About £1.60.) When I get home I'll give most of it to mum – she has to pay the rent on Friday. Then we'll have bean stew, as usual. Then I'll crash out on my mat on the floor. Tomorrow is another busy day.

▲ Pedro, aged 14.

An unequal society

Brazil is rich in natural resources. It is developing quite fast. But it has a big problem: **inequality**. Some people are very wealthy. Millions are very poor.

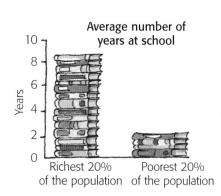

Average number of years at school

Each person here represents 10% of Brazil's population. So 20% of the people own 61% (or nearly two-thirds) of its wealth.

1% of the population owns almost half of Brazil's land. And millions of rural families have no land, and are forced to work for big landowners.

On top of that, Brazil's poorest people don't have much education. So they have even less chance of improving their lives.

The roots of this inequality lie deep in the past. Portuguese kings gave out huge tracts of land in Brazil as gifts and rewards to people. The new landowners got slaves to work on the land at first, for no pay. When slavery was abolished they hired workers, but paid them very little.

Today the landowners' families still own the land, and have got richer and richer. Their workers have not.

Did you know?
* In Brazil, around 1.4 million children under 15 work for a living.

Did you know?
* In Brazil, thousands of children live and sleep on the streets ...
* ... and around 3 a day are murdered.

Making things fairer

Brazil's government is trying to make life fairer. It is buying land from big landowners and sharing it out to poor people, with money to help them start farming. But the process is slow, and there's a long way to go.

Your turn

1 Make a large table to compare Barbra and Pedro's day. You could do it like this:

	Barbra	Pedro
morning	breakfast of ...	

2 *Why* has Barbra ended up with a more comfortable life than Pedro? Try to suggest some reasons.

3 Compare these pie charts for Brazil and the UK.

How wealth is distributed

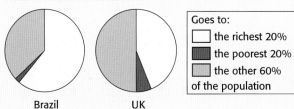

Goes to:
☐ the richest 20%
■ the poorest 20%
▨ the other 60%
of the population

Brazil   UK

a Is there inequality in the UK? Explain.
b Which has a more unequal society, Brazil or the UK?

4 *The Brazilian government is giving land, and help, to poor people, for farming.*
Arrange these boxes as a flow chart, to show how that will help to make Brazil a more equal society.

> They can also grow extra food, to sell.

> Poor people get land, and help, to start farming.

> Now they can grow food to feed their families.

> So they can get good jobs when they grow up.

> So their children won't have to go out to work.

> So they can go to school instead.

> So they will earn money.

5 The government is also setting up better schools, in poor areas. Make up your own flow chart, with at least four boxes, to show how this will help reduce inequality.

Brazil's rainforest

Here you'll learn more about Brazil's rainforest, and the threats to it.

The rainforest

Brazil has the largest area of rainforest in the world. It is part of the Amazon rainforest, that crosses 9 countries in South America. Brazil's share is about 14 times the size of the UK.

Who lives there?

Over 200 000 **indigenous** people, the Indios, live in Brazil's rainforest. They are the descendants of the Indios that lived in Brazil long long before the Portuguese arrived.

There are many different tribes. They live in scattered groups. Some hide deep in the forest, and live by hunting and fishing, without any contact with the modern world.

Lots of poor farmers also live there. By law, if they clear land and live on it for 5 years, they 'own' it. Over 150 000 poor families have gained land this way. There are also some very large farms and cattle ranches. Ranchers gain rights to use land just by clearing it, and moving cattle in.

There are many towns, and some cities, in and around the rainforest. Some started as Portuguese forts. Many grew thanks to trade in timber and rubber. The map on page 129 shows where the cities are.

What is happening to it?

Rainforest is being destroyed all over the world. Some reports say that an area the size of 5000 football fields is lost in Brazil *every day*. These photos show the causes – and some consequences.

At the start, logging was the main cause of rainforest loss. The timber was mostly exported.

Poor farmers clear rainforest to grow food for their families. It's called **slash and burn**.

Big farmers have cleared large areas for cattle ranches. Brazil is the world's top beef exporter.

Soya bean plantations are the latest threat. Brazil is the world's top soya bean exporter.

This satellite image shows how deforestation spreads. It often starts along tracks and roads that have been cleared by logging companies.

Men of the Guarani tribe protest in 2004, against a cattle ranch set up on their tribal land. Ranchers shot one man dead, and injured four others.

A place of conflict

Even though most of it is empty, there is a great deal of conflict in the rainforest. Violence and murder are common.

◆ The government has set aside land for the indigenous people. But ranchers, and illegal loggers and miners, invade it.

◆ The government has forbidden logging in most areas. But there is plenty of illegal logging – and the loggers often carry guns.

◆ Poor farmers have been chased off their land by soya farmers.

◆ Crooked lawyers help rich farmers to claim land that's not theirs.

◆ Some big farmers and cattle ranchers promise poor people jobs. They bring them to isolated farms. Then they treat them as slaves, and don't pay them.

◆ Meanwhile, other countries protest at the loss of the rainforest. (But still buy rainforest meat, timber, and soya!)

The government sometimes sends in the army and police, to stop illegal activities. But, in such a huge forest, they can't be everywhere.

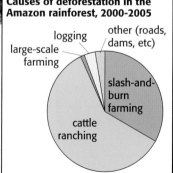

Animals are driven out or killed off when the rainforest is destroyed. They can't protest.

Your turn

1 Look at the satellite image at the top of this page.
  a What do you think the dark green shows?
  b What do you think the brown lines are?
  c Why are so many of the brown lines straight?
  d What is the white stuff in the top right corner?

2 Many different groups are in conflict, in Brazil's rainforest. See how many you can list.

3 It's hard to keep law and order in the rainforest. Why?

4 Now look at this pie chart.
  a What it it about?
  b Write at least four statements saying what you have learned from it. Use terms like *most*, *least*, *more than*, *not much*.
  As an extra challenge, see if you can give rough %.

Causes of deforestation in the Amazon rainforest, 2000-2005

logging
other (roads, dams, etc)
large-scale farming
slash-and-burn farming
cattle ranching

The challenges facing Brazil

In this unit you'll learn about Brazil's hopes for the future – and explore how one plan may threaten the rainforest.

Life will be better for everyone.

Our hopes for the future
- ◆ No more poverty
- ◆ A good education for all
- ◆ A fair society

All this will cost us a fortune!

Brazil's hopes for the future

Brazil is rich in resources. It is developing quite fast. But 1 in 5 of its people live in poverty. They have little or no education. And there is great inequality: a small % of people own much of Brazil's wealth.

Brazil wants to solve these problems. To do so, it needs a lot of money. It hopes to earn it by growing more crops, and finding more minerals, and making more goods, to sell to other countries.

So Brazil says it needs ...

To produce more crops and goods, and export more, Brazil says it needs:

- ◆ more dams, to give more electricity for industry (and homes)
- ◆ more farmland – and especially for rearing cattle, and growing crops like soya beans, that can earn Brazil a lot
- ◆ more exploration for oil, gas, and metal ores
- ◆ more roads, railways and waterways, to transport crops and other goods to ports – and around the country.

But the dilemma is ...

How can Brazil do all that AND protect the rainforest? Think about it:

- ◆ The rainforest covers 40% of Brazil. (50% is half.)
- ◆ It has big rivers suitable for dams.
- ◆ It's rich in other resources too (metals, diamonds, some gas and oil).
- ◆ It could provide a huge amount of farmland.
- ◆ The best route to the coast, to export beef and crops, is up through the rainforest to the River Amazon. Then cargo boats carry goods along the Amazon.

▲ *Soya beans. Used in making cereal, biscuits, ice cream, chocolate, pizzas, soap, and thousands of other things. But mostly in animal feeds.*

Some people say the government must exploit the rainforest, to help Brazil develop. Others say this would be a crime. The government is trying to find a balance.

▶ *Right: A road through the rainforest. It's called the BR-163. It is 1760 km long, and partly paved (as here).*

▶ *Far right: But most of the BR-163 is just a track. It often gets flooded, so lorries can get stuck for days.*

One rainforest project

This map shows the rainforest in 2000, and the paved roads in it. (There are also lots of dirt tracks.)

The government has big plans up its sleeve for new roads, and railways, and dams, in the rainforest.

One plan is going ahead already: to pave all of the BR-163 (so that it's more like a major road in the UK).

Look at the BR-163 on the map.

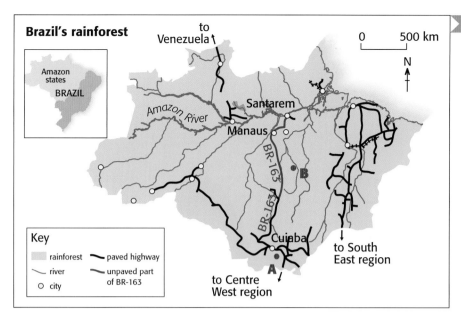

Protecting the rainforest

At the same time, the government is trying to protect the rainforest:

◆ It has set aside large areas that are not to be touched by anyone.

◆ It is getting tougher on illegal logging. (You can still cut down trees in some areas, but you need a permit.)

◆ By law, cattle ranchers must now leave 80% of their ranches forested.

◆ The government wants small farmers to stop slash-and-burn farming. And instead, to stick with land that is cleared already, and try to improve the soil, rather than clear new land.

The government will use satellite images to keep an eye on the rainforest.

▼ The state of the rainforest in 2000. Compare it with the map above. What do you notice?

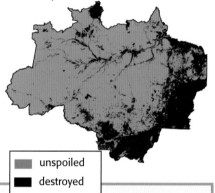

unspoiled
destroyed

Your turn

1 Look at Brazil's hopes for the future, at the top of page 128. Is it right to want these things?

2 Protesters say that roads lead to rainforest destruction.
  a Can you see any evidence of this, in the photos and maps on pages 127 – 129? If yes, present it!
  b Now see if you can *explain* the link between roads and rainforest destruction.

3 This is about the plan to pave all of the BR-163.
  a Why is it such an important road? Check the map.
  b Make a *large* table with headings like this:

① Affected	② Will gain because …	③ Will lose because …	④ Overall impact

  c Now look at the list on the right. The first entry is farmers growing soya beans, at **A** on the map above.
    i Will paving all of the BR-163 affect them? If *yes*, write *farmers* in column ① in your table.
    ii Will they gain? If *yes*, explain why in column ②.
    iii Will they lose in any way? If you think so, explain why, in column ③.

  d Repeat c for all the other people in the list.
  e For each group, or person, in your table, decide whether the *overall* impact is positive or negative. If positive write a ✓ in column ④. If negative write a ✗.

4 Now turn to page 60, and read about rainforests and global warming, Does it change your mind about any of your answers for question 3? Explain.

5 You are the Minister of the Environment. You want the rich countries to pay Brazil to protect the rainforest. Write a speech you will make to the United Nations. Say how the money will be used. (Page 61 may help.)

Will paving all of the BR-163 affect them?

farmers at **A** on the map, growing soya beans for export

poor Brazilians looking for a patch of land to farm

the residents of Manaus

people living in the UK

a small tribe of Indios, living at **B**

Pedro (page 124)

London, your capital city

The big picture

This chapter is about London, your capital city. These are the big ideas behind the chapter:

◆ London is a big exciting city – and it's your capital.

◆ It is made up of the City of London and 32 boroughs.

◆ Different areas of London are important for different things.

◆ London has a big ethnic mix, with some parts more mixed than others.

◆ Tube and street maps will help you plan your journeys in London.

Your goals for this chapter

By the end of this chapter you should be able to answer these questions:

◆ Where exactly is London, in the UK?

◆ What river runs through it?

◆ How did London start?

◆ About how many people live in London? About how many travel in to work there, every day?

◆ How is London organized?
(Mention the City, Greater London, and the boroughs.)

◆ London has some special areas, with their own names.
What can I say about the areas in this list?

*Westminster   the City of London   the West End   the East End
the South Bank   South Kensington   Knightsbridge*

◆ What does *ethnic diversity* mean?

◆ What can I say about the pattern of ethnic diversity in London?

◆ What's the Tube map like? In what ways is it different to street maps?

And then ...

When you finish this chapter, come back to this page and see if you have met your goals!

Did you know?
◆ London is the 25th largest city in the world.

Did you know?
◆ London's biggest business is finance.

Did you know?
◆ London is over 7 times bigger than our second largest city, Birmingham.

What if...
◆ ... rising sea levels drowned much of London?

What if...
◆ ... Birmingham was our capital city?

No, the Queen is not at home.

Your chapter starter

The photo on page 130 shows part of London.

Have you been there?

It's a capital city. What does that mean?

What's that river called?

Do you recognise anything in the photo?

Your capital city

Here you'll find out how London started, and explore some data about its population.

Your capital city

population: 7.7 million, or 12.7% of the UK population

contribution to the UK's wealth: 19%

non-white population: 29%

daily commuters from outside London: around 750 000

secondary schools: around 660

hospitals: around 80

cinemas: around 110

premiership football clubs: 5

shops: thousands

places to eat: thousands

So how did it start?

2000 years ago, London was just marshy ground beside a big river, the Thames. And empty except for some Britons living in huts.

It did not really start until the Romans invaded Britain, in 43 AD. At first, they made Colchester their capital. But they brought goods in by boat along the Thames. And soon a settlement grew around the bridge where the boats docked. They called it Londinium.

The settlement grew fast. And, some time after 100 AD, the Romans decided to make it their capital, instead of Colchester.

By 407 AD, the Roman army had left Britain. Londinium went downhill. By 450 it was almost empty. But its location was good. So by 600 AD, it had started growing again. In time, the Vikings arrived … then the Saxons … then the Normans. And the rest is history.

▲ *Heading for Londinium?*

▲ *We think Londinium looked like this, in 124 AD. It had a wall to defend it, and one bridge. Part of the wall is still standing.*

▶ *London today. It covers an area of 1610 sq km. Now there are 23 bridges over the river (not counting rail bridges). One (London Bridge) is very close to where the Roman bridge was.*

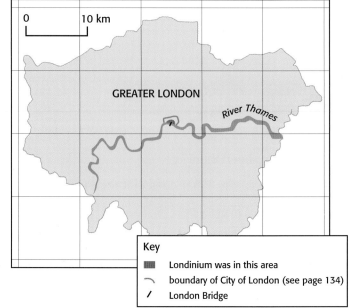

0   10 km

GREATER LONDON

River Thames

Key

▦ Londinium was in this area

⌐ boundary of City of London (see page 134)

∕ London Bridge

A multicultural city

Over the centuries, people came to London from all over the world. Since World War II, many different groups have arrived. So today, London is a big, lively and exciting city, with people of every race under the sun.

Over 300 different languages are spoken by pupils in London schools.

London's ethnic mix

Group	% of population
White British	60
White other	11
Mixed race	3
Black Caribbean	5
Black African	5
Black other	1
Indian	6
Pakistani	2
Bangladeshi	2
Chinese	1
Other Asian	2
Other	2

Your turn

1 Where is London?

2 About how wide is London at its widest part? (Scale!)

3 There are many good things about London's location, that helped it to grow. See how many you can identify. The maps at the back of this book may help.

4 Now you are going to draw a graph of the population since the year 1600, when Elizabeth I was queen.
   a Draw axes like the ones started below. The vertical axis shows the population, in millions. Continue it up to 8 million, and label it. (Try to use graph paper.)

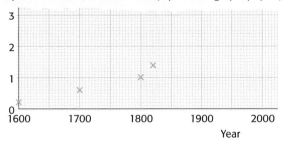

   b On your graph, plot the points for the data below. (Four points are shown above, to help you.)

Year	Population (millions)	Year	Population (millions)
1600	0.2	1940	8.6
1700	0.6	1950	8.2
1800	1.0	1960	8.0
1820	1.4	1970	7.5
1840	1.9	1980	6.8
1860	2.8	1990	6.8
1880	4.8	2000	7.2
1900	6.5	2006	7.7

   c Then join the points with a smooth curve, and give your graph a title.

5 This is about the graph you drew in question 4.
   a Is this statement true, or false? Give your evidence.
      i The population of London is larger now than ever.
      ii The population continues to decline.
   b When did the population grow fastest? Why do you think that was? (Think history!) Where do you think most of the people came from?
   c The population started to fall around 1940. See if you can come up with one reason.
   d The population is now rising again. Can you think of any reasons?

6 Look at this bar chart for age groups in London.

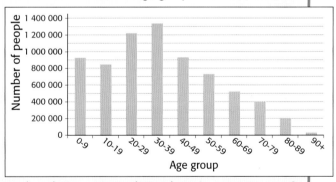

   a About how many people are there, in your age group?
   b There are more people aged under 10 than aged 10 to 19. See if you can explain why.
   c Which two age groups are the largest? Why do you think that is?

7 Look at the list showing ethnic mix, at the top of this page.
   a Which group are these most likely to belong to?
      i a person from Vietnam   ii an Irish person
      iii a Kenyan   iv a Jamaican
      v an Australian   vi a black American
   b Think of a good way to display the information from the list. (Bar chart? Pie chart? On a map?) Then do it!

What's London like?

Here you'll find out about the structure of London, and some different areas in it.

The City, and Greater London

Look at the map below.

◆ The small red area in the centre is called the **City of London**. It is London's finance centre. It stands just where Londinium was.

◆ **Greater London** is all of the coloured area. It is the City of London plus 32 districts or **boroughs**. The green lines show their edges. Each is run by a borough council.

Some places you may want to visit

This map of London shows some well-known venues. Which ones have you heard of? And some well-known areas are shaded. Match their labels (A to G) to the text boxes, to find out more.

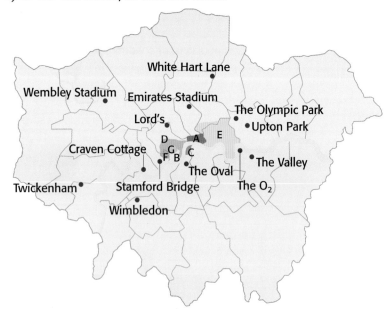

A   The City of London

◆ It's the finance centre. It has the Stock Market, the Bank of England, and lots of financial businesses.
◆ It is the world's top finance centre.
◆ It creates 4% of the UK's wealth.

B   Westminster

◆ It's the political centre, where Parliament is.
◆ The Prime Minister also lives here, in 10 Downing Street.
◆ And the Royal Family has a base here – Buckingham Palace, below.

D   The West End

◆ It's a big shopping centre. Oxford Street and Bond Street are here.
◆ It's also an entertainment centre, with theatres, cinemas and clubs.

C   The South Bank

◆ It is a centre for theatre, concerts, and the arts.
◆ The London Eye and the London Aquarium are here too.

F South Kensington

◆ If you want some top museums, this is the place to go.
◆ It has the Natural History Museum, the Science Museum, and the V&A.
◆ The Royal Albert Hall is here too.

E The East End

◆ This area has lots of street markets, and old pubs. (Like *EastEnders*?)
◆ Many immigrants settled here, so it has a rich ethnic mix.

G Knightsbridge

◆ Here you'll find some very posh shops … like this famous one.

Your turn

1 Look at the places marked on the map on page 134. How much can you say about them? Have a go!

2 Is the City of London a city? Explain.

3 Look at the seven areas, A to G. If you had to choose just two to visit, which would they be? Why?

4 Now turn to page 130. The photo includes two of the areas A to G. Which two? (Look for clues!)

5 See if you can explain why the West End and East End have those names.

6 Look at the map and list of names, on the right. Using these and the map on page 134, see if you can work out which borough this is in:
   a Wembley stadium   b Lord's cricket ground
   c Arsenal FC   d Wimbledon tennis courts
   e the O₂ concert venue f Twickenham rugby stadium

7 Now see if you can name:
   a three boroughs that are part of inner London
   b four boroughs that border the River Thames
   c three boroughs that form part of the outer suburbs

8 Some parts of London are more racially mixed than others. They have greater **ethnic diversity**.
   Look again at the map on the right. Is this true or false?
   a The borough of Brent has high ethnic diversity.
   b Bromley is more ethnically diverse than Islington.
   c The City of London has a high racial mix.
   d Chelsea FC is in an area of low ethnic diversity.

9 The areas of high ethnic diversity tend to be in clusters. Why do you think that is?

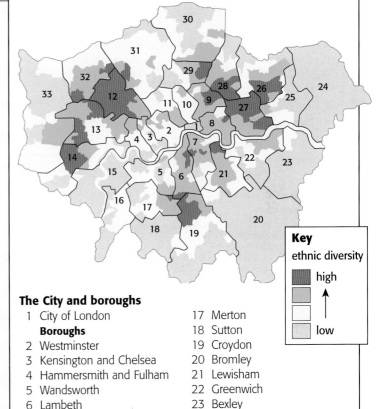

Key
ethnic diversity

| high |
| |
| |
| low |

The City and boroughs

1 City of London
   Boroughs
2 Westminster
3 Kensington and Chelsea
4 Hammersmith and Fulham
5 Wandsworth
6 Lambeth
7 Southwark
8 Tower Hamlets
9 Hackney
10 Islington
11 Camden
12 Brent
13 Ealing
14 Hounslow
15 Richmond-upon-Thames
16 Kingston-upon-Thames

17 Merton
18 Sutton
19 Croydon
20 Bromley
21 Lewisham
22 Greenwich
23 Bexley
24 Havering
25 Barking and Dagenham
26 Redbridge
27 Newham
28 Waltham Forest
29 Haringey
30 Enfield
31 Barnet
32 Harrow
33 Hillingdon

Your day out in London

Here you'll have a great day out, in London, with the help of two maps.

Getting around

Get ready for an exciting day out in London. For part of the day, you'll be in the area shown in the photo on page 130. You will use the two maps in this Unit to help you get around. Compare the photo and maps. (The yellow dot on the photo marks Westminster Tube station.)

The Tube map

The Tube (or Underground) is a great way to get around London. Over 3 million people use it every day. Think about that!

Below is part of the Tube map. It's really a diagram, not a map to scale. The coloured lines are different Tube lines. The key shows their names.

▲ *You'll go by Tube.*

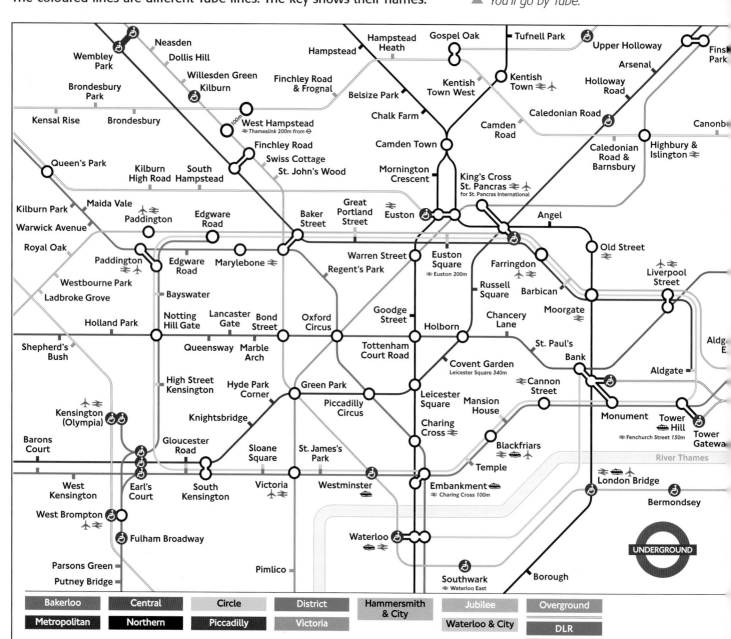

Bakerloo	Central	Circle	District	Hammersmith & City	Jubilee	Overground
Metropolitan	Northern	Piccadilly	Victoria	Waterloo & City		DLR

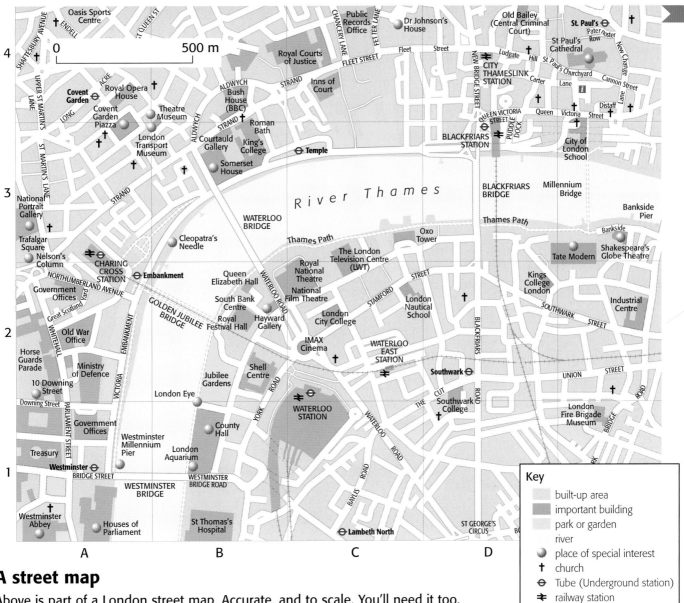

The map shows part of central London including the River Thames, with labelled streets, stations and places of interest.

Key
- built-up area
- important building
- park or garden
- river
- place of special interest
- ✝ church
- ⊖ Tube (Underground station)
- ⇌ railway station
- ┼┼┼┼ railway
- main through roads
- other streets

A street map

Above is part of a London street map. Accurate, and to scale. You'll need it too.

Your turn

It's your day out in London. How exciting! The list on the right shows what you plan to do. You will arrive by train, at Paddington station. And from there, take the Tube.

1 a Find Paddington and Westminster on the Tube map.
  b Decide on your Tube route from Paddington to Westminster. (Four Tube lines go through Paddington.) Name the line(s) you will use, and the stations you will go through. Say why you chose that route.

2 a Now, using your list and the street map, see if you can draw a sketch map of your route from Westminster Tube station to St Paul's Tube station.
  b On your map, mark in all the places you visited.

3 Then decide which Tube lines you will take, to go:
  a from St Paul's to Oxford Circus, to go shopping
  b from Bond Street Tube station (it's on Oxford Street) to Paddington, to get your train back home.

My day out
- arrive Paddington
- take Tube to Westminster
- look at Houses of Parliament
- cross bridge and go to London Aquarium
- go up London Eye
- go back across bridge, and take boat up river from Westminster Millennium pier to Bankside pier
- go into Tate Modern, look around, and have lunch
- cross Millennium Bridge to St Paul's Tube station
- from there take Tube to Oxford Circus
- go shopping along Oxford Street
- take Tube from Bond Street Tube station to Paddington
- get train home

Ordnance Survey symbols

ROADS AND PATHS

M I or A 6(M)	Motorway
A 35	Dual carriageway
A 31(T) or A 35	Trunk or main road
B 3074	Secondary road
	Narrow road with passing places
	Road under construction
	Road generally more than 4 m wide
	Road generally less than 4 m wide
	Other road, drive or track, fenced and unfenced
	Gradient: steeper than 1 in 5; 1 in 7 to 1 in 5
Ferry	Ferry; Ferry P – passenger only
	Path

PUBLIC RIGHTS OF WAY

(Not applicable to Scotland)

1:25 000	1:50 000	
		Footpath
		Road used as a public footpath
+++++++		Bridleway
		Byway open to all traffic

RAILWAYS

	Multiple track
	Single track
	Narrow gauge/Light rapid transit system
	Road over; road under; level crossing
	Cutting; tunnel; embankment
	Station, open to passengers; siding

BOUNDARIES

+ — + — + —	National
+ + + + +	District
— · — · — · —	County, Unitary Authority, Metropolitan District or London Borough
	National Park

HEIGHTS/ROCK FEATURES

50	Contour lines
· 144	Spot height to the nearest metre above sea level

outcrop cliff scree

ABBREVIATIONS

P	Post office	PC	Public convenience (rural areas)
PH	Public house	TH	Town Hall, Guildhall or equivalent
MS	Milestone	Sch	School
MP	Milepost	Coll	College
CH	Clubhouse	Mus	Museum
CG	Coastguard	Cemy	Cemetery
Fm	Farm		

ANTIQUITIES

VILLA	Roman	✗	*Battlefield* (with date)
Castle	Non-Roman	✻	*Tumulus/Tumuli* (mound over burial place)

LAND FEATURES

ruin	Buildings
	Public building
	Bus or coach station
} Place of Worship {	with tower / with spire, minaret or dome / without such additions
∘	Chimney or tower
	Glass structure
Ⓗ	Heliport
△	Triangulation pillar
	Mast
	Wind pump / wind generator
	Windmill
+	Graticule intersection
	Cutting, embankment
	Quarry
	Spoil heap, refuse tip or dump
	Coniferous wood
	Non-coniferous wood
	Mixed wood
	Orchard
	Park or ornamental ground
	Forestry Commission access land
	National Trust – always open
	National Trust, limited access, observe local signs
	National Trust for Scotland

WATER FEATURES

Marsh or salting · Towpath Lock · Slopes · Cliff · High water mark · Aqueduct Canal · Ford · Flat rock · Low water mark · Weir Normal tidal limit Sand · Lighthouse (in use) · Bridge Dunes · Beacon · Lake Footbridge · Lighthouse (disused) · Shingle · Mud

========= Canal (dry)

TOURIST INFORMATION

P	Parking
P&R	Park & Ride
V	Visitor centre
i / i	Information centre
✆	Telephone
⨯	Camp site/ Caravan site
⚑	Golf course or links
	Viewpoint
PC	Public convenience
⨯	Picnic site
	Pub/s
M	Museum
	Castle/fort
	Building of historic interest
	Steam railway
	English Heritage
✻	Garden
	Nature reserve
	Water activities
	Fishing
☆	Other tourist feature

138

Map of the British Isles

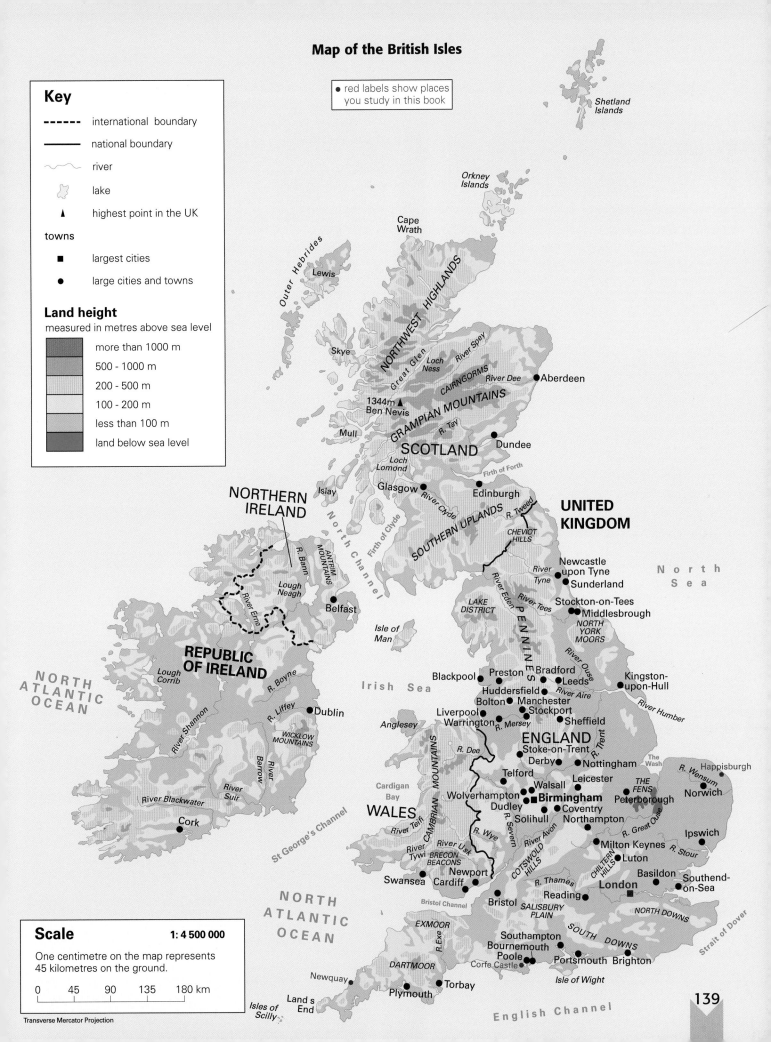

● red labels show places you study in this book

Key

- - - - - international boundary
——— national boundary
〰〰 river
🝝 lake
▲ highest point in the UK

towns
■ largest cities
● large cities and towns

Land height
measured in metres above sea level

more than 1000 m
500 - 1000 m
200 - 500 m
100 - 200 m
less than 100 m
land below sea level

Scale   1 : 4 500 000

One centimetre on the map represents
45 kilometres on the ground.

0   45   90   135   180 km

Transverse Mercator Projection

Shetland Islands

Orkney Islands

Cape Wrath

NORTHWEST HIGHLANDS

Outer Hebrides

Lewis

Skye

Great Glen

Loch Ness

River Spey

CAIRNGORMS

River Dee

● Aberdeen

1344m ▲ Ben Nevis

GRAMPIAN MOUNTAINS

R. Tay

Mull

SCOTLAND

● Dundee

Loch Lomond

Firth of Forth

Islay

Glasgow ■

River Clyde

Edinburgh ●

R. Tweed

UNITED KINGDOM

Firth of Clyde

SOUTHERN UPLANDS

CHEVIOT HILLS

North Channel

ANTRIM MOUNTAINS

R. Bann

Lough Neagh

River Erne

NORTHERN IRELAND

Belfast ●

REPUBLIC OF IRELAND

Lough Corrib

R. Boyne

R. Liffey

Dublin ●

WICKLOW MOUNTAINS

River Shannon

River Barrow

River Suir

River Blackwater

Cork ●

NORTH ATLANTIC OCEAN

St George's Channel

Isle of Man

Irish Sea

Anglesey

CAMBRIAN MOUNTAINS

WALES

Cardigan Bay

River Teifi

River Tywi

BRECON BEACONS

Swansea ●

Cardiff ●

Newport ●

R. Usk

R. Wye

Newcastle upon Tyne ●

River Tyne

Sunderland ●

Stockton-on-Tees ●

Middlesbrough ●

NORTH YORK MOORS

River Eden

River Tees

LAKE DISTRICT

PENNINES

River Ouse

Blackpool ●

Preston ●

Bradford ●

Leeds ●

Kingston-upon-Hull ●

River Aire

River Humber

Huddersfield ●

Bolton ● Manchester ●

Liverpool ● Stockport ●

Warrington ● R. Mersey

Sheffield ●

R. Dee

ENGLAND

Stoke-on-Trent ●

R. Trent

Derby ● Nottingham ●

Telford ●

Leicester ●

THE WASH

R. Wensum ● Happisburgh

Walsall ●

Wolverhampton ●

■ Birmingham

Dudley ●

Coventry ●

Solihull ●

Northampton ●

THE FENS

Peterborough ●

Norwich ●

R. Great Ouse

Ipswich ●

Milton Keynes ●

R. Stour

CHILTERN HILLS

Luton ●

R. Severn

River Avon

COTSWOLD HILLS

Basildon ●

Southend-on-Sea ●

London ■

Reading ●

R. Thames

NORTH DOWNS

Bristol ●

Bristol Channel

SALISBURY PLAIN

SOUTH DOWNS

Strait of Dover

EXMOOR

R. Exe

Southampton ●

Bournemouth ●

Poole ●

Corfe Castle ●

Portsmouth ●

Brighton ●

Isle of Wight

DARTMOOR

Newquay ●

Land s End

Isles of Scilly

Plymouth ●

Torbay ●

NORTH ATLANTIC OCEAN

North Sea

English Channel

— international boundary
• capital city

abbreviations
BELG.   BELGIUM
B-H.   BOSNIA-HERZEGOVINA
C.   CROATIA
CENT. AF. REP.   CENTRAL AFRICAN REPUBLIC
CZ.   CZECH REPUBLIC
F.   FYROM
                 (Former Yugoslav Republic of Macedonia)
K.   KOSOVO
L.   LIECHTENSTEIN
LITH.   LITHUANIA
MT.   MONTENEGRO
LUX.   LUXEMBOURG
NETH.   NETHERLANDS
S.   SLOVENIA
SE.   SERBIA
SL.   SLOVAKIA
SWITZ.   SWITZERLAND
U.A.E.   UNITED ARAB EMIRATES
U.S.A.   UNITED STATES OF AMERICA

Equatorial Scale 1: 95 000 000

Did you know?
◆ The Earth is 4600 million years old.
◆ It weighs 6000 million million million tonnes.

Arctic Circle

Alaska (U.S.A.)

GREENLAND (Den.)

C A N A D A

Nuuk (Godthåb)

U. S. A.

Ottawa

Washington D.C.

Azores (Port.)

Bermuda (U.K.)

Tropic of Cancer

Hawaiian Is. (U.S.A.)

MÉXICO

México

Havana

Nassau

THE BAHAMAS

CUBA

HAITI   DOMINICAN REPUBLIC

JAMAICA   Kingston

Puerto Rico (U.S.A.)

ST. KITTS-NEVIS
ANTIGUA & BARBUDA
DOMINICA
ST. LUCIA

CAPE VERDE IS.

Belmopan
BELIZE

GUATEMALA   HONDURAS
Guatemala   Tegucigalpa
San Salvador
EL SALVADOR   NICARAGUA
Managua
San José   Panamá
COSTA RICA
PANAMA

ST. VINCENT & THE GRENADINES
BARBADOS
GRENADA
TRINIDAD AND TOBAGO

Caracas

VENEZUELA

GUYANA

Georgetown   Paramaribo
SURINAME   Cayenne
FRENCH GUIANA (Fr.)

Bogotá

COLOMBIA

Equator

Galapagos Is. (Ec.)

Quito
ECUADOR

P
E
R
U

B R A Z I L

Tokelau Is. (N.Z.)

SAMOA   American Samoa (U.S.A.)

French Polynesia (Fr.)

Lima

Brasília

La Paz

BOLIVIA

TONGA   Niue (N.Z.)   Cook Is. (N.Z.)

Tropic of Capricorn

Pitcairn Is. (U.K.)

PARAGUAY

Asunción

C
H
I
L
E

A
R
G
E
N
T
I
N
A

URUGUAY

Santiago

Buenos Aires   Montevideo

Falkland Is. (U.K.)
Stanley

South Georgia (U.K.)

The continents and oceans

North America

NORTH ATLANTIC OCEAN

Europe

Asia

PACIFIC OCEAN

PACIFIC OCEAN

Africa

South America

SOUTH ATLANTIC OCEAN

INDIAN OCEAN

Oceania

SOUTHERN OCEAN

Antarctica

Amazing – but true!

◆ Nearly 70% of the Earth is covered by saltwater.
◆ Nearly 1/3 is covered by the Pacific Ocean.
◆ 10% of the land is covered by glaciers.
◆ 20% of the land is covered by deserts.

World champions

◆ Largest continent – Asia
◆ Longest river – The Nile, Egypt
◆ Highest mountain – Everest, Nepal
◆ Largest desert – Sahara, North Africa
◆ Largest ocean – Pacific

Did you know?

The world has:
◆ over 200 countries
◆ nearly 7 billion people
◆ over 6000 different languages.

Glossary

A

acid rain – rain that has acidic gases dissolved in it; it can kill fish and plants

adapt – change to suit the conditions; plants have adapted to suit the climate

adult literacy rate – the % of people aged 15 and over who can read and write a simple sentence

air mass – a huge block of air moving over the Earth; it can be warm or cold, damp or dry, depending on where it came from

air pressure – the weight of air pressing down on the Earth's surface

altitude – height of a place above sea level

anemometer – use it to measure wind speed

arch – the curved outline left when the sea erodes the inside of a cave away

atmosphere – the gas around the Earth

B

barometer – it's for measuring air pressure

bay – a smooth curve of coast between two headlands

beach – an area of sand or small stones, deposited by waves

beach replenishment – you add sand to a beach to replace the sand the waves have carried away

biodiverse – has many different species of plants and animals

biofuel – a fuel made from plant material

biome – a very large ecosystem; all the hot deserts together make up one biome

birth rate – the number of births in a country in a year, per thousand people

built environment – all the built things around us: buildings, streets, bridges, and so on (not the natural environment)

burglary – breaking into a building to steal

buttress roots – large roots that grow partly above the ground, to support tall trees

C

carbon-neutral – overall, does not add extra carbon dioxide to the air

carnivore – eats animals

CCTV – closed circuit television, used in shops and on streets to fight crime

climate – the 'average' weather in a place; what the weather is usually like there

climate change – how climates around the world are changing, because of the rise in average air temperatures

cloud cover – how much of the sky is hidden by cloud; given in eighths (oktas)

coast – where the land meets the sea

coastal defences – barriers to protect the coast from erosion or flooding

common assault – hitting or threatening to hit someone

compensation – money you receive to make up for a loss or harm you suffered

convectional rainfall – caused by the sun heating the ground, which in turn heats the air; the air rises and its water vapour condenses to form clouds

crime – an action that breaks the law

criminal – someone who commits a serious crime, or lives a life of crime

D

death rate – the number of deaths in a country in a year, per thousand people

decomposers – they break down dead and waste material in an ecosystem; worms and bacteria are examples

defensible space – a space that people can watch over and protect from criminals

deforestation – cutting down forests

delta – flat area of deposited material at the mouth of a river, where it enters the sea

densely populated area – lots of people live there

deposit – to drop material; waves deposit sand and small stones in sheltered parts of the coast, forming beaches

depression – a weather system made up of two fronts, a warm front chased by a cold one; it brings wet windy weather

designing out crime – you design new housing estates and other buildings to make them as crime-proof as possible

developed country – it has good public services and a high standard of living

development indicator – a measure you use to check how developed a country is; for example, its adult literacy rate

domestic violence – violence in the home; for example a man punching his wife

E

economic – to do with money and finance

ecosystem – a natural unit made up of living things and their non-living environment; for example a forest, a desert

emissions – waste gases and dust particles we let into the air, from power stations, car exhausts and so on

environment – everything around you; the air, soil, water, and climate form the environment in an ecosystem

environmental crime – an action such as illegal dumping of harmful waste in rivers

erosion – wearing away of rock, stones and soil by rivers, waves, the wind or glaciers

ethanol – an alcohol made from plant material; it burns well so is used as fuel

ethnic diversity – there are many different ethnic groups in the place

exports – things a country sells to other countries

F

favela – a slum in a South American city

fertiliser – you add it to soil to help crops grow; it contains nutrients they need

fetch – the length of water the wind blows over, before it meets the coast

forgery – faking a document or signature

fossil fuels – coal, oil and natural gas (they are the remains of plants and animals that lived millions of years ago)

fraud – making false claims, usually in order to make money

front – the leading edge of an air mass; a warm front means a warm air mass is arriving

frontal rainfall – rain caused when a warm front meets a cold one

fuels – thing we use to provide energy; we usually burn them (but not nuclear fuel)

G

GDP (gross domestic product) – the total value of the goods and services produced in a country, in a year

GDP per capita – a country's GDP, divided by the population; it's a measure of how wealthy the people are

global warming – the way average temperatures around the world are rising

greenhouse gases – gases that trap heat around the Earth

groynes – barriers of wood or stone down a beach, to stop sand being washed away

H

headland – land that juts out into the sea

herbivore – an animal that eats only plants

hunter gatherers – live by hunting animals and collecting fruit and seeds

hydroelectricity – electricity generated when a river spins a turbine

I

imports – things that are bought in from other countries

Indigenous people – they are descended from the people who first settled there

Indios – the native 'Indians' whose ancestors were the first settlers in Brazil

inequality – the unequal sharing of wealth in a society

infant mortality – how many babies out of every 1000 born alive, who die before their first birthday

infrastructure – the basic services and facilities in a country: electricity supply, water supply, road network and so on

isolated – quite far from others

L

latitude – how far a place is north or south of the equator, measured in degrees

life expectancy – how many years a new baby can expect to live, on average

logging – cutting down trees for timber

low – another word for a depression

longshore drift – how sand and other material is carried parallel to the shore, by the waves

M

mental map – a map that you carry in your head; it might not be very accurate !

meteorologist – a person who studies weather and climate

mugging – attacking a person in the street in order to steal something

multicultural – has many ethnic groups

N

National Grid – the network of power stations and cables that supply our electricity

Neighbourhood Watch – a scheme where neighbours keep an eye on each others' homes to help prevent crime

nomadic – moves from place to place (for example with animals, for grazing)

non-renewable resource – a resource we will run out of one day; for example oil

North Atlantic Drift – a warm current in the Atlantic Ocean; it keeps our west coast warmer in winter

nuclear fuel – has unstable atoms that break down, giving out lots of energy

nutrient – a substance needed for growth, and to stay healthy; for example plants need nitrogen compounds

O

ocean currents – currents of water in the ocean, that are warmer or colder than the water around them

offender – a person who commits a crime (often used for young people under 18)

P

permafrost – the ground under the surface that is permanently frozen, in the tundra

photosynthesis – the process in which plants make their food from carbon dioxide and water; it needs sunlight

population – the number of people living in a place

population density – the average number of people per square kilometre

population distribution – how people are spread around, in a country or area

population pyramid – a bar graph showing the population, divided into males and females in different age groups

precipitation – water falling from the sky; it could fall as rain, hail, sleet or snow

prevailing wind – the wind that blows most often; in the UK it is a south west wind (it blows *from* the south west)

primary sector (of the economy) – where people earn a living by collecting things from the Earth (farming, fishing, mining)

pull factors – factors that attract people to a place (for example, better wages there)

push factors – factors that push people out of a place (for example, no work there)

PV (photovoltaic) cell – a cell that converts sunlight into electricity

R

radiation – harmful rays and particles given out by some substances; radiation can cause cancer, and a big dose can kill you

relief – the differences in height of the land

relief rainfall – rain caused when air is forced to rise over a hill or mountain

renewable resource – a resource that we can grow or make more of; for example wood

resources – things we need to live, or use to earn a living; for example food, fuel

rural area – an area of countryside, where people live on farms and in villages

S

salt marsh – a low-lying marshy area by the sea, with salty water from the tides

secondary sector (of the economy) – where people earn a living by making things (usually in factories)

secure accomodation – a type of prison for young offenders

sentence – the punishment for a crime

shingle – small pebbles

slash and burn farming – farmers chop down and burn vegetation to clear land for crops; when the soil is worn out they move on

smelting – the process of getting metals from their ores

social – about people and society (while *economic* is about money and finance)

solar power – power we get by using sunlight as a fuel, for example in PV cells

sparsely populated area – very few people live there

spit – a strip of sand or shingle in the sea

stack – a pillar of rock left standing in the sea when the top of an arch collapses

stump – the remains of an eroded stack

sustainable – can be carried on without harming people's quality of life, or the economy, or the environment

T

target hardening – installing things to make it harder for criminals to get at their targets (for example steel shutters)

temperature – how hot or cold something is, measured in degrees Centigrade

terrorism – violent acts (such as bombings) carried out for political reasons

tertiary sector (of the economy) – where people earn a living by providing services (for example doctors, teachers, reporters)

thermometer – for measuring temperature

tidal range – the fall in sea level from high to low tide

tides – the rise and fall in sea level, due mainly to the pull of the moon

toxic – poisonous

traffic offences – offences to do with driving and parking vehicles

transport – the carrying away of material by rivers, waves, the wind or glaciers

tropics – the area between the Tropics of Cancer and Capricorn (that is, between 23.5 °N and 23.5 °S of the equator)

U

undernourished – does not get enough food nutrients

urban area – a built-up area, such as part of a city; it's the opposite of rural

V

vandalism – damaging things on purpose; for example smashing up phone boxes

vegetation – all the trees and other plants growing in a place

victim – a person against whom a crime is committed

visibility – how far you can see; on a foggy day in could be just 1 or 2 metres

W

wave-cut notch – a notch cut in a cliff face by the action of waves

wave-cut platform – the flat rocky area left behind when waves erode a cliff away

weather – the state of the atmosphere at any given time

weathering – the breaking down of rock; it is caused mainly by the weather

wind – air in motion

wind direction – the direction the wind blows *from*

wind farm – a group of wind turbines set up to generate electricity from the wind

wind speed – how fast the wind is blowing

wind vane – it shows the wind's direction

Index